Improving My Vocabulary

Dr. V.P. Gupta

M.Sc. Ph. D. (Chemistry) EPPAM (Manchester)
Formerly Prof. of Chemistry NCERT,
and
WORLD Bank Team Member (DPEP Project)

Editor – Usha Gupta

Technical Advisor – Yashasvi Ghadale

INDIA · SINGAPORE · MALAYSIA

ISBN 979-8-89066-874-5

Contents

Preface

After passing class 5 from govt. Primary school Deepalpur in 1957 with distinction, I took admission in Sanskrit High School, Bahalgarh, about 3 km from Deepalpur (Sonipat) in class 6 and started writing the alphabets of the English language on a four line notebook. Initially, the second language seemed interesting to me while learning simple words like, 'Bat', 'Cat', 'Tap', 'Dog' 'Cup', 'Not', 'Net', but started facing problems while writing and pronouncing words like 'No' and 'Know' in the same way but 'To' and 'Go' in different ways. We were asked by our English teacher to write many new words in our notebook with their meanings in Hindi, our mother tongue and do practice for spellings of various words given by the teacher. After learning spellings of English words but without any knowledge of phonetics of the language, I passed class 6 with distinction in all subjects including English but with many doubts and queries in my mind about pronunciation. My English teachers from class 7-10 in Hindu High School were excellent in grammatical part of the language but none laid emphasis on phonetics as none of them were the product of any missionary school. I passed class 10 examination conducted by Panjab University, Chandigarh by securing 79 % marks and 80 % in English, and earning the "National Merit Scholarship" from Govt. of India.

I faced music in first year class in Chemistry in the degree college, when I failed to distinguish the pronunciation of words like "Chopra", "Cheese" and 'Chemistry'. All teachers delivered lectures in English but I faced problems in writing my papers in English language. My score went down from 79 percent in class 10 to 60.1 percent in Pre University class of Panjab University. The same was the case with my classmates, though we had earned a National Merit Scholarship from Govt. of India. This is the common problem of students coming from the rural settings and studying in Hindi medium or regional languages schools. The problem can be solved to some extent by start reading some English newspapers, magazines and biographies of eminent personalities, watching English news/channels and make a list of new words with their meanings by consulting dictionaries, Google and Wikipedia. I started subscribing to 'Hindustan Times' from my college days. Spoken and English writing improved year after year with learning of thousands of new words till my post graduation in Chemistry from Kurukshetra University. I started delivering my lectures in English in Hindu College Sonipat (Panjab University) and later in colleges of NCERT – the national level body of Govt. of India looking after the school education of the country and also during teacher training programs conducted by NCERT and Regional Institutes of Education, earlier known as Regional Colleges of Education. While writing my autobiography in 2017 – 2020, I learnt a few new words in introduction part written by Pankaj (Bobby) Gupta and Foreword by Dr. B.L. Khandelwal the former Prof. and Head of chemistry department at IIT, Delhi, Emeritus Prof. CSIR, and director of many institutes of repute later. I was amazed to read the write up of some excursion by Anshul Jadhav, studying in school in Newcastle (Australia) during his school holidays after 2nd term, when I had to consult the dictionary to know the meaning of some words used by that student in Australia.

I got interested to read the book entitled, "Exam Warriors "written by our Prime Minister, Shri Narendra Modi in which he suggested students to improve their vocabulary by learning at least 30 new words daily. I was thus motivated to compile a list of new words unknown to me for the help of students like me. In a way, this will be more appropriate to mention that the young boy and the above two stalwarts of their field are the real motivators for me to take up this project. I am extremely grateful to above teachers of mine for the initiation process and also to Bobby Gupta, Shuchita Gupta, Naren Goel and Rashmi Goel of the U. S., Dr. Kavita Gupta Ghadale of Indore and to Deepika Jadhav and Vineet Jadhav of Newcastle, Australia to provide me an opportunity to read many books from their library corner during my stay there. For the last two years I was busy in compiling a list of words, some of which are very common (marked with stars) and many new words taken from books, newspapers published from India and the U.S. and Times of India published from Bhopal and San Francisco Chronicle published from San Francisco.

I am sure that the common words marked with star will be useful for school/college going students in day to day communication, whereas new words may help readers to improve their vocabulary and may be helpful to youths preparing for MBA and other competitive examinations. The text also includes sentence formation from some words in between. These exemplar sentences are framed with the view to develop social values in readers. American English is followed throughout the text. As I did, consultancy of dictionaries of English to English/Hindi/regional languages, Google/Wikipedia may further prove useful to students and learners for use of English language in day to day life to enhance their skills in reading, writing, comprehending and in drafting work besides their better and purposeful interactions with their peers and seniors, as English is still the link language of the world until Hindi replaces English.

Dr. V.P. Gupta 30 June 2023

Foreword

It took me by surprise when Dr. V. P. Gupta, my earlier professor asked me to write the foreword for his book "Improving my Vocabulary". My association to Dr. Gupta goes back to the year 1982 when I took admission in B.A B.Ed. four-year course in Regional College (R.I.E.) Bhopal, a constituent unit of NCERT, MHRD, GoI. Being visually impaired, I was trying hard to accommodate myself in the new environment but Dr. Gupta was one of the few professors who instilled confidence in me. He was always concerned about me and encouraged me to fly high in life. Since then, he has seen me growing in my career.

In today's world, a strong vocabulary is essential for success in both academic and professional settings. However, for learners of a second language, vocabulary acquisition can be a challenging and daunting task. The present book is easy to follow and supplies a wealth of information that will help learners of English reach their language learning goals. It is a comprehensive and effective guide to vocabulary building for young and the old alike. This book is different from other books of the kind because words found in newspapers and books by Indian and foreign authors used in day-to-day life in India, the U.S. Australia and U. K. have been chosen. The title of the book is self explanatory to improve vocabulary of the readers, especially those who don't have English as their mother tongue or who got school education in a language other than English.

The book covers a wide range of topics, including words of common use and new words with their meanings in English. In addition to its comprehensive coverage of vocabulary building, the readers will find it a well written and engaging work to them. Dr. Gupta has used clear and concise language and supplied many examples by including a few exemplar sentences with the view to develop some social values. It will be worthwhile for the readers to make an attempt to make sentences after learning difficult words in real life situations.

This book is not only a valuable resource for anyone who wants to communicate effectively in English, but also is especially relevant and useful for Indian and other learners preparing for various competitive examinations. I highly recommend this book to anyone who is serious about improving their English vocabulary.

Dr. Rohit Trivedi
M.A. English, Ph.D.
Professor of English, Sarojini Naidu Govt. Girls'
P.G. (Autonomous) College, Bhopal, India.

Acknowledgements

I am highly thankful to Dr. B. L. Khandelwal, Prof. of Chemistry and former Head of Chemistry department, IIT Delhi, Emeritus Scientist, CSIR, Govt. of India and Director of many Institutes of repute for writing foreword of my Autobiography in Sep. 2020 and acquainting me with many new words. In Pankaj Gupta, a versatile engineer and the former Managing Director, International Business of Virsec in Silicon Valley in the U.S. I found an encyclopaedia of English words which made me aware of many new words. Anshul, a 12 year old boy studying in year 6 in some missionary school of Newcastle in Australia three years ago mesmerized me, when I had to consult the dictionary to check meanings of some words used by him in his description of some excursion with his parents in 2020 school holidays. When I came across these new words even after learning the English language for the last 58 years, it came to my mind to compile some words used by us in daily conversation and new words used by authorities of the English language like Adam Grant and our PM Narendra Modi in “Exam Warriors”, Sagarika Ghose of “Times of India”, “San Francisco Chronicle” published from Silicon Valley of the U.S., “The Golden Book of the Holy Vedas”, “Shiva Stories and Teachings From the Shiv Mahapuran” by Vijay Goel, translated by A. A. Macdonald. H. Oldenberg and F. MaxMuller, “Krsna” by A. C. Bhaktivedanta Swami Prabhupada, “The Discovery of India” by Jawaharlal Nehru, first PM of India, “Biography of Indira Gandhi”, the former Prime Minister of India by Sagarika Ghose, and many other books. I express my heartfelt gratitude to my above three teachers, all authors and publishers of the above books and newspapers for selecting words, some of which are commonly used. Such words are marked with stars which can be quite helpful to readers in their daily conversation with their peers and for interaction with friends and officials. I consulted the Oxford English Dictionary, Google and Wikipedia for writing meaning of many words not known to me earlier. It is my great pleasure to express my hearty thanks to the Oxford dictionary, Google, Wikipedia, and publisher of all books and the above newspapers for including meanings of the new words for the benefit of readers who want to improve their vocabulary of the English language from this text.

I am also grateful to all heads of academic institutions, students and many other intellectuals from different sectors of society to give me a chance to apprise me about their opinion before publication of this book. I am highly thankful to Mrs Usha Gupta for editing the manuscript and for her valuable suggestions from time to time, Mr. Namit Agrawal for initial editing, Ms Yashasvi Ghadale of IIT Delhi and Master Ayush Ghadale for technical help during development of the Book. I am deeply indebted to my wife Usha for taking her time and bearing me during writing of this book and to all children and grandchildren for their motivation and support from the very beginning of undertaking this project. I am also thankful to Notion Press agreeing to be my publishing partner and giving the present shape to the book.

Dr. V.P. GUPTA 30 June, 2023

Pre-Publishing Views

(Based on different sets of 10 words given to each subject)

- Abhishek Gupta, Sr. Project Manager, Newgen Software Limited, NOIDA, India – A great initiative. Words seem interesting and looking forward to using them in day to day activities.
- Amod Sharma, Sr. Lecturer in English, Sainik School, Rewa, M.P. India – Many words are new to me in spite of teaching English for more than 28 years. This compilation will be of great help to school and college going children.
- Anand Dwivedi, IRSSE, GoI, Ahmedabad – This task by Dr. Gupta is laudable for development of communication skills of students and youth.
- Anshul Jadhav, year 9 student, Merewether School, Newcastle, NSW, Australia – This is a great list of words. I know 7 of them.
- Aryan Gupta, B S 1st year UCB California – A great effort by Dr. Gupta. This will be very useful to high school kids to increase their vocabulary for SAT examinations.
- Ayush Ghadale, class 11 student, DPS, Indore, India – I know a few words. This will help school and college going children.

- Bharat Gupta, BE, MBA, Cambridge – Director, Operational Risk, Barclay Bank, London – Very good compilation of words. 8 words known to me. Will definitely be helpful to youths in general to improve their level of English language.
- Bobby Pankaj Gupta, Founder and CEO Infused. ai., Silicon Valley, California – compilation of words taken from different Biographies/books of eminent authors known over the globe is a praiseworthy task by Dr. Gupta for improving communication skills of readers of all ages.
- Deepak Gupta, Advisory Manager for Cyber security, Dallas, USA – This compilation of words is the result of tireless research of many years. I only know 4 out of 10 words but they are rarely used in conversation. Will help school, college and university going youths.
- Dr. Deepika Jadhav, Sr. Consultant John Hunter Hospital and Director Ishana Well – Being Center, Newcastle, NSW, Australia – Got a chance to have a glance at a few words, which are quite new. Will be helpful to learners to improve their vocabulary. Best read a book.
- Dhruv, class 11 student, DPS Indore, India – I know only a few words. These will help school and college going students.
- Dr. Jyoti Rathore, Govt. P.G. College of Education, Khandwa, India – Words of common use and new

words will be of immense use to my students in improving their communication skills in English.

- Dr. Kavita Gupta Ghadale, Sr. Consultant Obs., Gynae and Laparoscopic Surgeon Bombay Hospital Indore, India – A great piece of work for improving English vocabulary of youths and readers of all ages including doctors and health workers.
- Dr. L. N. Pandey, Principal (retd) Govt Higher Secondary School, Rewa, India – The new words will help students, teachers and Youths of rural areas to improve their vocabulary for better communication skills.
- Dr. Pushpa Chauksey, Principal, Govt. Hamidia P.G. College, Bhopal, India – Many words are new even to me. This compilation will definitely be helpful in improving communication skills of students, teachers and youths in general.
- Dr. Rohit Trivedi, Prof. of English, Govt.Sarojini Naidu P.G. College Bhopal – Words Marked with stars will be useful in day to day interaction. The other ones will be useful to youths preparing for MBA and other competitive examinations.
- Dr. Vineet Jadhav, Director, Edgeworth Family Practice, Newcastle, NSW, Australia – A great compilation of new words for improving vocabulary. I will feel pleasure in recommending it for my patients.

- Ishana Jadahav, year 5 student, Bishop Anglican College, Newcastle NSW, Australia – These words are very helpful. I learnt many of them. May help a lot of students like me.
- Kiran Gupta, Principal, S.M. Hindu Higher Secondary School, Sonipat, India – Words marked with star will be helpful to school going children. The other ones may help UG and PG students for MBA and other competitive examinations.
- Kunal Gupta, B S, UCB, Sr. Software Engineer, Data Science Strim Inc., Silicon Valley, California, USA – Wonderful but I know 90 percent of them. A very useful list of new words for learners of the English language.
- Namit Agrawal, Sr Consultant, IBM, NOIDA, India – I have gone through hundreds of words. Will help even the technocrats in improving their communication skills.
- Navidha Agrawal, class 10 student, The Khaitan School, NOIDA, India – This is a great set of words. I think it would be very useful to students not only in writing their thesis and essays but also in improving our day to day life also.
- Nitu Gupta, Sr. Principal Consultant, Genpact Headstrong Capital Market, NOIDA, India – Many words are new to me. Should be useful to school and college going students.

- Narendra Goel, Sr Advisor and CFO, Cyber Security and IT Companies, Orange County, LA, USA – Had a look at some exemplary words. 7 words are in my use quite often. Hope this helps school and college going youths.
- O.P. Kapoor, CMD, MP Tourism (retd). Bhopal – A highly literary work by Dr. Gupta. Will help school/ college going youths.
- Preeti Gupta, Sr. PGT in Physics, Hindu Vidyapeeth, Sonipat, India – Really New Words. Definitely this will help.
- Shashidhar Kapur, Independent Journalist and Filmmaker, Ex – Channel Head, ETV (MP/CG), Ex – Features Editor, HT, Bhopal – Perhaps words like proletariat, Anthropomorphic and benediction are less useful for those students whose first language is not English. The remaining seven words would be of great value addition to the students' vocabulary.
- Shuchita Gupta, CTO (Health Care) IBM, Silicon Valley, California – Great Work. Very good sample list of words. Will be very useful for all ages.
- Usha Gupta, English Teacher, Anand Vihar School (retd), Bhopal – Words marked with stars will be useful to school going children. Others may improve the communication skills of all ages of students and youth.

- Vihan Gupta – class 6, Cannon Lane Primary School, Pinner, London, UK – A good list of words. I know the meaning of 6 words. Will be highly useful to students.
- Yashasvi Ghadale, B. TECH, IIT Delhi – All the words are great. Would be helpful for a lot of people.

Author's Note and words (Part A and Part B) – Words Marked with stars may be useful in day to day interaction. The others may help you for MBA/competitive examinations. American English is followed in the text. Try to learn 5 new words daily.

PART A

Abdicate (v). – (of a monarch) Renounce one's throne.

Abject* (adj.). – Terrible and without any hope; without any pride or respect for yourself.

Accentuate (v). – Make it more noticeable or prominent.

Accost (v). – Go up and talk to a stranger in a way that's rude or frightening.

Accretion* (n). – Growth or increase by the gradual accumulation of additional layers or matter; a thing formed or added by gradual growth or increase; ASTRONOMY – The coming together and cohesion of matter under the influence of gravitation to form large bodies.

Acme (n). – The point at which something is at its best or most highly developed.

Acumen* (n). – The ability to make good judgments and make quick decisions.

Adage* (n). – A proverb or short statement expressing a general truth.

Adroitly* (adverb). – Not serious; silly.

Affable* (adj.). – Pleasant, friendly and easy to talk to.

Afloat* (adj.) – Floating in water; not sinking.

Aggrandize (v). – Increase the power, rank or wealth of a person or country.

Agitprop (n). – Political (original communists), especially in art or literature.

Ambit* (n). – The scope, extent or bounds of something.

Amnesia* (n). – A partial or total loss of memory.

Amphibian (n). – A sea plane, tank, or other vehicle that can operate on land and on water; a cold blooded vertebrate anima of a class that comprises the frogs, toads, newts, salamanders, and caecilians.

Amygdale (n). – A roughly almond – shaped mass of gray matter inside each cerebral hemisphere, involved with the experience of emotions.

Anal (adj.) – Relating to or situated near the anus.

Anklet girded (n). – A sock that reaches just above the ankle, an ornamental circlet worn around the ankle.

Anoint (v). – Smear or rub with oil, typically as part of a religious ceremony, rub something with (any other substance)

Appertain (v). – Relate to; concern; be appropriate or applicable, belong or be connected as a rightful part or attribute.

Aqueduct (n). – A structure like a bridge for carrying water across a valley or low ground.

Archaic* (adj.) – Very old or old – fashioned.

Astute (adj.). – Clever/good at judging people/situations.

Avid(adj.). – Very enthusiastic about something (usually a hobby).

Baiter* (n). – A person who causes continuous pain/ distress/annoyance to another.

Balk (v). – Hesitate or be unwilling to accept an idea or undertaking; (n). – A roughly square timber beam.

Ballad* (n). – A long song/poem about love.

Barter* (v). – Exchange (goods or services) for other goods or services without using money; (n). – The action or system of bartering.

Bastille (n). – Any prison or jail, especially one conducted in a tyrannical way, a fortified tower, as of a castle; a small fortress; citadel.

Bequeath* (v). – Leave (property) to a person or other beneficiary by will; pass (something) on or leave (something) to someone else.

Bigot* (n). – A person with very strong and unreasonable beliefs or opinions and who will not listen to or accept a different opinion.

Bigotry* (n). – Obstinate or intolerant devotion to one's own opinions and prejudices.

Bizarre. (adj.). – Very strange or unusual.

Blabber. (adj.). – Relating to or characteristic of an artisan.

Blasphemous (adj.). – Sacrilegious, showing lack of respect for God or to a religion.

Blather. (v). – Talk in a long winded way without making much sense, (n). – Long winded talk with no real sense.

Blaze* (n). – A very large and dangerous fire, a very bright show of light or color.

Blight (v). – Spoil or damage something.

Bludgeon (n). – A thick stick with a heavy end, used as a weapon; (v). – Beat (someone) repeatedly with a bludgeon or another heavy object.

Boat – rocker*.(n). – One that rocks the boat; one who challenges the status quo as an unreconstructed boat rocker.

Bounteous* (adj.). – Generously given; bountiful.

Brood (v). – Worry or to think a lot about something that makes you worried or sad; (used about a female bird) to sit on her eggs.

Buffet*(n). – a meal consisting of several dishes from which guests serve themselves; a room or counter in a station, hotel, or other public buildings selling light meals or snacks.

Calcify* (v). – Harden by deposition of or conversion into calcium carbonate or another insoluble calcium compound.

Caliphate*(n). – The rule or reign of a caliph or chief Muslim ruler; the area ruled by a caliph.

Calumny (n). – The making of false and defamatory statements about someone in order to damage their reputation; slander.

Carping*(adj.). – Difficult to please; critical.

Cathartic (adj.). – Providing psychological relief through the open expression of strong emotions; causing catharsis; MEDICINE – purgative; (n). – A purgative drug used for constipation.

Caucasian (n). – A member of any of the races who have pale skin.

Cede*(v). – Give up (power or territory).

Chaff* (v). – Tease

Clam* (n). – A type of fish that can be beaten.

Colic* (n). – Pain in the stomach area, which especially babies get.

Condescend(v). – Show that one feels superior.

Consternation (n). – A feeling of shock or worry.

Contemplation* (n). – Viewing, ticking.

Contort (v). – Move or to make something move into a strange or unusual way.

Contravene* (v). – Break a law or a rule.

Convivial (adj.). – (of an atmosphere or event) Friendly, lively, and enjoyable; (of a person) cheerful and friendly; jovial.

Creaky* (adj.). – Old – fashioned or decrepit.

Culinary (adj.) – Connected with cooking.

Damning* (adj.). – Criticizing something very much. "It is always better to look at the positive aspect of happenings around us rather than damning them:

Debonair* (adj.). – Confident, stylish, and charming (typically used by a man); urbane.

Defanged* (adj.). – Rendered harmless or ineffective.

Delinquent (adj.). – (typically of a young person) Tending to commit crime, particularly minor crime; FORMAL – failing in one's duty.

Delirium (n). – A mental state where somebody becomes delirious, an uncontrolled state or situation, agitation, aberration, frenzy.

Delve (v). – reach inside a receptacle and search for something; ARCHAIC – dig; excavate.

Despicable (adj.). – Very unpleasant or evil.

Destigmatize (v). – To remove shame or disgrace from.

Detestable. (adj.). – Deserving to be hated or criticized, abhorrent.

Discerning (adj.). – Able to recognise the quality of somebody/something.

Domineering (adj.). – Asserting one's will over another in an arrogant way.

Don* (v). – Put on (an item of clothing).

Douse* (v).. – Pour a liquid over; drench; extinguish.

Dredge* (v). – Clear the mud, etc. from the bottom of a river, canal etc. using a special machine.

Dungeon (n). – (from a French word donjon meaning Inner tower in a castle) a dark, usually underground prison.

Dupe* (v). – To lie to somebody in order to make him/her believe something or do something.

Ecstasy* (n). – An overwhelming feeling of great happiness or joyful excitement, an emotional or religious frenzy or trance – like state.

Edifice*(n). – A large imposing building, a complex system of beliefs.

Effulgence (n). – The ability to shine brightly.

Enmesh*.(v). – Involve (someone) in a difficult situation from which it is hard to escape.

Ensconce.(v). – Establish or settle (someone) in a comfortable, safe place.

Ephemeral (adj.). – lasting for a very short time.

Epilogue* (n). – A section or speech at the end of a book or play that serves as a comment on or a conclusion to what has happened.

Epithet (n). – An adjective or phrase used to describe somebody/something's character or most important quality, especially in order to say something good or bad about.

Equanimity (n). – A calm state of mind which means that you don't become angry or upset, especially in difficult situations, composure.

Eschew* (v). – Deliberately avoid using; abstain from.

Euphoria* (n). – (listen) is the experience of pleasure or excitement and intense feeling of well – being and happiness.

Fallacious* (adj.). – Based on mistaken belief.

Fierce* (adj.). – Having or displaying an intense or ferocious aggressiveness; (adverb). – INFORMAL – IRISH – Very; extensively.

Figurative (adJ.). – (used about a word or expression) not used with its exact meaning but used for giving an imaginative description or a special effect.

Filial (adj.). – Relating to or due from a son or daughter; BIOLOGY – Denoting the offspring of a cross.

Finesse* (n). – Impressive delicacy and skill.

Firmament* (n). – The heavens or sky.

Flail (v). – wave or swing wildly; beat or flog.

Flamboyant (adj.). – (of a person or their behavior) tending to attract attention because of their exuberance, confidence, and stylishness.

Flotsam (n). – The wreckage of a ship or its cargo found floating on or

Fracas (n). – A noisy disturbance or quarrel.

Fret (v). – Worried and unhappy about something.

Funken (v). – Sparkle; flammen.

Gag* (v). – Choke or retch; put a gag on (someone).

Ghettoize (V). – Put in or restricted to an isolated or segregated place, group or situation.

Gospel* (n). – One of the four books in the Bible that describe the life and teachings of Jesus Christ.

Graffiti*(n). – Pictures/writings on a wall in public life.

Harbinger (n). – A forerunner of something; a person or thing that announces or signals the approach of another.

Hemp (n). – A pleasant that is used for making rope and rough cloth and for producing an illegal drug (cannabis).

Hoary (adj.). – Grayish white; overused and unoriginal.

Howl* (v). – Make a good loud sound.

Idolatry* (n). – The worship of idols, extreme admiration, love, or reverence for something or someone.

Ignoble (adj.). – Not honorable in character or purpose; of humble origin or social status.

Imbue (v). – Fill somebody or something with deep feelings, strong opinions or ideas, or a particular sense of value or equality.

Immaculate (adj.). – Perfectly clean and tidy; without any mistakes; perfect.

Impeccable* (adj.). – In accordance with the highest standards, faultless, RARE THEOLOGY – Not liable to sin.

Imperious*(adj.). – Arrogant or domineering.

Impetuous* (adj.). – Acting or done quickly and without thinking.

Implacable (adj.). – Unable to be appeased or placated; unable to be stopped; relentless.

Imprimatur* (n). – A person's authoritative approval; an official license issued by Roman Catholic Church to print an ecclesiastical or religious book

Impunity*(n). – Exemption from punishment or freedom from the injurious consequences of an action.

Inanity* (n). – A nonsensical remark or action; silliness.

Inchoate (adj.). – Just begun and so not fully formed or developed; rudimentary.

Incognito (adverb). – Hiding your real name and identity (especially if you are famous and do not want to be recognized.

Incontrovertible* (adj.). – Convert one into the other.

Incursion* (n). – Sudden attack by foreign armies etc., usually across international borders.

Indefatigable (adj.). – FORMAL – Never giving up or getting tired of doing something.

Indemnify(v). – Reimburse, compensate, repay.

Indignation* (n). – Anger or annoyance provoked by what is perceived as unfair treatment.

Indomitable (adj.). – Impossible to subdue or defeat. “Do you think that you are indomitable?”

Indubitable(adj. – Impossible to doubt; unquestionable.

Inextricably (adverb). – In a way that is impossible to disentangle or separate.

Infallible* (adj.). – Never failing, always doing what you are supposed to do, (used about a person) never making mistakes or being wrong.

Inkling* (n). – A slight feeling (about something).

Innuendo (n). – An allusive or oblique remark or hint, typically a suggestive or disparaging one.

Innuendo (n). – An indirect way of talking about somebody/ something, usually suggesting somebody bad or rude.

Insatiable. (adj.). – That cannot be satisfied; very great, demanding, insistent, desiring, gluttonous, greedy, pressing, unpleasable.

Insinuation* (n). – An unpleasant hint/suggestion.

Insomnia* (n) – Inability to sleep.

intercede*.(v). – Intervene on behalf of another.

Interloper (n). – A person present in a situation or place where they do not belong to or do not have permission to be.

Intransigence (n). – Refusal to change one's views or to agree about something.

Intrepid* (adj.). – Without any fear of danger.

Intrinsically* (adverb) – In a natural character.

Intubate* (V). – Insert a tube in to (a person or a body part, especially the trachea for ventilation.

Invertebrate (n). – An animal without a solid line of bones.

Invocation (n). – Formal – The act of making somebody feel a particular emotion or remember something.

Irreconcilable* (adj. – FORMAL. – (used about people or their ideas and beliefs) So different that they cannot be made to agree.

Itinerant (adj.). – Traveling from place to place.

Jab* (v). – Pierce/push/inject with a sharp object.

Jock (n). – Disc jockey; NORTH AMERICAN – An enthusiast or participant in a specified activity.

Jokester* (n). – a person fond of making or telling jokes.

Joust* (v). – Compete, especially for power or control.

Kinaesthetic (adj.). – Relating to a person's awareness of the position and movement of the parts of the body by means of sensory organs (proprioceptors) in the muscles and joints.

Lacklustre (adj.). – (force or conviction of the hair or the eyes), Not shining, dull; lacking in vitality, force or conviction; uninspired or uninspiring.

Laconic. (adj.). – Using or involving the use of a minimum of words, concise to the point of seeming rude or mysterious.

Laicite (n). – Secularity (French).

Languish* (v). – Be forced to remain in an unpleasant place or situation(of a person, animal or a plant), lose or lack vitality, grow weak.

Languishing*(adj.). – Failing to make progress or be successful.

Leviathan (n). – A very large aquatic creature, especially a whale; a thing that is very large or powerful, especially an organization or vehicle; (in biblical use) a sea monster, identified in different passages with the whale and the crocodile.

Lexicon (n). – The vocabulary of a person, language, or branch of knowledge; dictionary, especially of Greek,

Hebrew, Syriac, or Arabic; the complete set of meaningful units in a language.

Libation (n). – A drink, a drink poured out as an offering to a deity.

Licking (n). – A heavy defeat or beating.

Limpid* (adj.). – (used about liquids, etc.) clear, (used about a style of writing, expression etc.) easily understood; clear.

Lorgnette (n) – A pair of glasses or opera glasses held in front of a person's eyes by a long handle at one side.

Lull* (v). – Make yourself relaxed and calm.

Mammon (n). – Wealth regarded as an evil influence or false object of worship and devotion.

Milieu*(n). – A person's social environment.

Mow* (v). – Cut grass using a machine (a mower), trim, and trump.

Muzzle (v). – Prevent (a person or group) from expressing their opinion freely.

Niche(n). – A job position etc. that is suitable for you.

Nix* (v). – Put an end to, cancel.

Numismatist* (n). – A person who collects or studies coins and medals.

Oblivious (adj.). – Not noticing or realizing what is happening around you.

Obsequies* (n). – Funeral rights, funeral service.

Onerous* (adj.). – (of a task or responsibility) Involving a great deal of effort, trouble, or difficulty; law involving heavy responsibility.

Opprobrium (n). – Harsh criticism or censure; public disgrace arising from shameful conduct; an occasion or cause of disgrace.

Ostensibly (adverb) – As appears or is stated to be true, though not necessarily so; apparently.

Outlier* (n). – A person or thing differing from all other members of the group or set.

Overtly (adverb). – Without concealment or secrecy; openly

Oviparous (adj.). – (used about animals) Producing eggs rather live babies

Pageant (n). – A type of public entertainment with people dressed in clothes from past times.

Paltry* (adj.). – Too small to be considered important or useful.

Paranoia (n). – Unjustified suspicion and mistrust of other people.

Pare down (v). – Reduce the size of something by cutting or shaving off its outer layers; trim something.

Parochial* (adj.). – Only concerned with small issues that happen in your local area and not interested in more important things.

Partisanship (adj.). – The quality or action of strongly supporting a person, principle, or political party often without judging or considering the matter carefully.

Passable* (adj.). – Good enough but not very good; (used about roads, rivers etc.) possible to use or cross; not blocked.

Penchant (n). – Something that you like very much to do.

Perennial (adj.). – (used about plants) Living for two years or more; that happens often or that lasts for a long time.

Petulance (n). – Insolvent or rude in speech or behavior.

Piquant*.(adj.). – Having a pleasantly sharp taste or appetizing flavor; pleasantly stimulating or exciting to the mind.

Pique (v). – Arouse (interest or curiosity); (n). – A feeling of irritation or resentment resulting from a slight, especially to one's pride.

Pithy (adj.). – (of language or style) Terse and vigorously expressive

Plumage (n). – A bird's feathers collectively.

Precocious (adj.). – (of a child) Having developed certain abilities or inclinations at an earlier age than is usual or expected; (of a plant) flowering or fruiting earlier than usual.

Predilection (n). – Especially something unusual.

Presumptuous (adj.). – Confident that something will happen or that somebody will do something without making sure first, in a way that annoys people.

Profligacy (n). – The trait of spending extravagantly, extravagance.

Profusion (n). – A very large quantity of something.

Prolific* (adj.). – (used especially about a writer, artist etc.) Producing a lot.

Propensity (n). – An inclination or natural tendency to behave in a particular way.

Protégé (n). – A person who is guided and supported by an older and more experienced or influential person.

Pugnacious (adj.). – Eager or quick to argue, quarrel, or fight.

Pulsate (v). – Move with strong regular movement.

Pun* (n). – A joke exploiting the different possible meanings of a word or the fact that there are words which sound alike but have different meanings.

Puritanical (adj.). – Having or displaying a very strict or censorious moral attitude towards self – indulgence or sex.

Ram (v). – Roughly force (something) into place; be very crowded.

Rambling (n). – The activity of walking in the countryside for pleasure; (adj.). – (of writing or speech) Lengthy and confused or inconsequential; (of a plant) putting out long shoots and growing over walls or other plants.

rampant.*(adj.). – (used about sth bad) Existing or spreading everywhere in a way that is very difficult to control.

Rancor (n). – Envy, enmity, hatred, malevolence, enmity.

Raucous (adj.). – Making or constituting a disturbingly harsh and loud noise.

Real politik (n). – A system of politics or principles based on practical rather than moral or ideological considerations.

Reap* ((v). – Cut or gather (a crop or harvest); harvest the crop from (a piece of land); receive, (especially something beneficial) as a consequences of one's own or another's action.

Receptacle (n). – A container for putting something in; the rounded area at the top of the stem that supports the head of a flower.

Recuse* (v) – (of a judge) Excuse oneself from a case because of a potential conflict of interest or lack of impartiality.

Refoulement (n). – The forcible return of refugees or asylum seekers to a country where they are liable to be persecuted.

Reminiscent (adj.). – That makes you remember somebody/ something; similar to.

Renege (v). – Go back on a promise, undertaking, or contract; another term for revoke; ARCHAIC – renounce or abandon.

Resplendent (adj.) – Brightly colored in an attractive and impressive way

Reticence (n). – Reserve; the quality of being reticent.

Retribution (n). – Punishment inflicted on someone as vengeance for a wrong or criminal act.

Riveting* (adj.). – Completely engrossing; compelling.

Salivate* (v). – Secrete saliva, especially in anticipation of food; display great relish at the sight of the prospect of something.

Salvage*. (v). – Rescue (wrecked or disabled ship or its cargo) from loss at sea.

Sanctum* (n). – A holy place; a private place or room where somebody can go and not be disturbed.

Sanguine. (adj.). – Blood re, optimistic or positive, especially in an apparently bad or difficult situation.

Sarcasm*(n). – An ironic or satirical remark tempered by humor.

Saute* (v). – (used about food) Fry food quickly in a little fat or oil until it turns brown.

Scourge (n). – A person or thing that causes a lot of trouble or suffering.

Secede* (v). – Withdraw formally from membership of a federal union, an alliance, or a political or a religious organization.

Seigneur (n). – A feudal lord; the lord of manor.

Servile (adj.). – Of or characteristic of a slave or slaves; having or showing an excessive willingness to serve or please others.

Shackles (n). – A pair of fetters connected together by a chain, used to fasten a prisoner's wrist or ankles together.

Sheaf* (n). – A bundle of grain stalks laid lengthwise and tied together after reaping; (v). – Bundle into sheaves.

Shorn* (n). – Trimmed, clipped or shaved.

Silage (n). – Grass or other green fodder compacted and stored in airtight conditions, typically in a silo, without first being dried, and used as animal feed in the winter; (v). – preserve (grass and other green fodder) as silage.

Skirting* (n). – A wooden board running along the base of an interior wall.

Slanderous* (adj.). – Magnificent and impressive in appearance.

Slink (v). – Move somewhere slowly and quietly because you don't want anyone to see you, often when you feel guilty or embarrassed.

Slipshod (adj.). – Characterized by a lack of care; worn out at the heels.

Slovenly* (adj.). – Lazy, careless and untidy.

Smother* (v). – Kill (someone) by covering their nose and mouth so that they suffocate.

Smudge* (v). – Cause (something) to become messily smeared by rubbing it; a blurred or smeared mark on the surface of something.

Smut(n). – A fungal disease of cereals in which parts of the ear change into black powder; (n). – A small flake of soot or other dirt or a mark left by one.

Snarl* (v). – (of an animal such as a dog) Make an aggressive growl with bared teeth; (n). – An act or so und of snarling.

Snob (n). – A person who believes that their tastes in a particular area are superior to those of other people.

Snobbery (n). – The character or quality of being a snob.

Snuff(n). – (especially in past times) Tobacco which people breathe up into the nose in the form of a powder.

Sorcerer* (n). – (in stories) A man with magical powers, who is helped by evil spirits.

Stingy* (adj.). – Mean; ungenerous.

Stolid (adj.). – (used about a person) Showing very little emotion or excitement.

Strewn (adj.). – Untidily scattered.

Stymie (v). – Prevent or hinder the progress of.

Suppliant (n). – A person making a humble or earnest request to someone in power or authority; (adj.). – Making or expressing a plea, especially to someone in power or authority.

Tandem* (n). – A bicycle with seats and pedals for two riders, one behind the other, (adverb). – With two or more horses harnessed one behind another; (adj.). – Having two things arranged one in front of the other.

Tantalize (v). – Excite the senses or desires of (someone), torment or tease (someone) with the sight or promise of something that is unobtainable.

Tawny (adj.). – Of a yellowish – brown or orange – Brown color.

Theocratic (adj.). – Relating to or denoting a system of government in which priests rule in the name of God or a god.

Thicket* (n). – A dense group of bushes or trees.

Tout (v). – Attempt to sell (something), typically by a direct or persistent approach; NORTH AMERICAN – Offer racing tips for a share of any resulting winnings.

Trample (v). – Walk on somebody/something and damage or hurt him/her.

Travesty (n). – A false, absurd, or distorted representation of something; (v). – Represented in a (false, absurd or distorted way).

Tumult (n). – A state of confusion or disorder; a loud confused noise, especially one caused by a large mass of people.

typically oval in shape, consisting of a portrait in profile carved in relief on a background of a different color.

Tyrannosaur (n). – A very large bipedal carnivorous dinosaur of the late Cretaceous period, with powerful jaws and small claws like front legs.

Udder (n). – The part of a female cow, etc. that hangs under its body and produces milk.

Unscathed* (adj.). – Not hurt, without injury

Usurp* (v). – Take somebody's position and/or power without having the right to do this.

Usurpation (n). – Annexation, confiscation, abduction, apprehension, arrest, arrogation, grab, preemption, seizure, snatch.

Vantage* (n). – A place or position affording a good view of something.

Vengeful (adj.). – Seeking to harm someone in return for a perceived injury.

Vetter* (n). – Someone who vets or checks.

Vile (adj.). – Very bad or unpleasant.

Virulent (adj.). – (of a disease or poison) Extremely severe or harmful in its effects; bitterly hostile.

Warped (adj.). – Deformed, distorted, contorted, turned from the natural, normal, or true direction, or character.

Whorl (n). – Loop, coil, hoop, a pattern of spirals or concentric circles.

Writhe.(v). – Turn and roll your body around.

PART B

Abattoir* (n) – BRITISH – Slaughterhouse.

Aberration* (n). – A departure from which is normal, usual, or expected, typically an unaware one; BIOLOGY – A characteristic that deviates from the normal type.

Abet* (v). – Encourage or assist (someone) to do something wrong, in particular to commit a crime; encourage someone to commit (a crime).

Abhor (v). – Regard with disgust and hatred, hate something very much.

Abhorrent (adj.). – Repugnant, inspiring disgust and loathing.

Ablution (n). – The act of washing yourself clean.

Abominable (adj.). – Very bad; shocking.

Abomination (n). – A thing that causes disgust or loathing, a feeling of hatred.

Abound*(v). – Exist in large numbers or amounts.

Abrasive*(adj.). – (of a substance or material) Capable of polishing or cleaning a hard surface by rubbing or grinding; showing little concern for the feelings of others; harsh.

Abreast* (adverb). – Next to or level with somebody/ something and going in the same direction, beside, in alignment, shoulder to shoulder.

Abrogate* (v). – Repeal or do away with (a law, right or formal agreement).

Abstraction* (n). – Formal – A general idea not based on any particular real person, thing or situation, the state about something and not paying any attention to what is happening around you, preoccupation.

Abstruse. (adj.). – Difficult to understand.

Abysmal* (adj.). – Extremely bad, appling; very deep.

Abyss (n) – A very deep hole that seems to have no bottom.

Ace* (n). – Playing card with single spot on it, ranked as the highest card in its suit in most card games; INFORMAL – A person who excels at a particular sport or other activity; (v) – (in tennis and similar games) Serve an ace against (an opponent).

Acerbic* (adj.). – Tasting sour or bitter; (especially of a comment or style of speaking) sharp and forthright.

Achilles heel (n). – A weakness or vulnerable point.

Acolyte* (n). – A person assisting a priest in a religious service or procession. "There are many acolytes besides the main priest in Hindu Temples".

Acquiesce (v). – Accept something reluctantly but without protest.

Acquiesce (v). – Accept something without argument, although you may not agree to it.

Acquiesce* (v). – Accept something without argument, although you may not agree with it.

Acreage* (n). – An area of land, typically when used for agricultural purposes, but necessarily measured in acres.

Acrimonious* (adj.). – (typically of speech or discussion) Angry and bitter.

Ad – hominem (adj.). – (of an argument or reaction) Directed against a person rather than the position they are maintaining.

Adage (n). – A proverb or short statement expressing a general truth.

Adamantine (adj.). – Unable to be broken.

Adjudicate* (v). – Make a formal judgment on a disposed matter; act as a judge in a competition.

Admonish* (v). – Tell somebody firmly that you don't approve of something that he/she has done; strongly advise somebody to do something.

Advent* (n). – The act of somebody/something arriving, (in the Christian year) the four weeks before Christmas.

Adversarial*.(adj.). – Involving or characterized by conflict or opposition.

Aeon (n). – An extremely long period of time; thousands of years.

Affable* (adj.). – Friendly, good – natured, or easy to talk to.

Afflict* (v). – Cause somebody/something to suffer pain, sadness, etc. trouble, trudge.

Aficionado (n). – A person who is very knowledgeable and enthusiastic about an activity; subject or pastime. "You will become an aficionado after learning the words of this booklet". Do you also feel this way ?"

Agility* (n). – Swiftness, briskness, dexterity, rapidity, etc.

Agitprop (n). – Political (original communist) propaganda, especially in art or literature.

Agnostic (n). – A person who believes that nothing is known of the existence or nature of God.

Agrarian (adj.). – Connected with farming and the use of land for farming.

Airpocalypse (n). – The presence of dense smog in many parts of Asia.

Aisle*(n). – A passage between the rows of seats in the theater, church etc.

Alacarte*.(n). – The practice of ordering individual dishes from a set menu in a restaurant .

Alacrity* (n). – Great willingness, eagerness or enthusiasm.

Alienated* (adj.). – Experiencing or inducing feelings of isolation or estrangement.

Allay (v). – Diminish or put at rest (fear, suspicion, or worry), relieve or alleviate (pain or hunger).

Allegory (n). – A story, play, picture etc. in which each character or event is a symbol representing an idea or a quality.

Alliance* (n). – An agreement between groups, countries, etc. to work – together and support each other.

Alliteration (n). – The occurrence of the same letter or sound at the beginning of adjacent or closely connected words.

Alon (n). – Oak tree (Hebrew).

Altruism* (n). – The fact of caring about the needs and happiness of other people more than your own.

Altruist (n). – A person unselfishly concerned for or devoted to the welfare of others (opposed to egoism).

Ambivalence* (n). – He state of having mixed feelings or contradictory ideas about something or someone.

Ambrosia.(n). – GREEK and ROMAN MYTHOLOGY – the food of the gods; a fungal product used as food by ambrosia beetles.

Ameliorate* (v). – Make something better.

Amnesiac (n). – A person experiencing a partial or total loss of memory.

Amoebiasis (n). – A parasitic infection of the colon with the amoeba, amoebic dysentery.

Amphitheater* (n). – A circular building without a roof and with rows of seats that rise in steps around an open space.

Amygdale (n). – A roughly almond – shaped mass of gray matter inside each cerebral hemisphere, involved with the experiencing emotions.

Anachronistic (adj.). – Antique, out – of – date, something old – fashioned, anything that bluntly clashes with the time in which it is seen.

Anarchist* (n). – A person who rebels against any authority, established order, or ruling power; vocalist, nihilist.

Anchorage* (n). – A place where boats and ships can anchor, a place where something can be fastened to something else.

Animism* (n). – The attribution of a living soul to plants; the belief in a supernatural power that organizes and animates the material universe.

Animosity* (n). – Strong hostility.

Animus (adj.). – A feeling of hate or anger towards someone or something.

Animus (n). – Hostility or ill feeling; motivation to do something.

Anodyne (adj.). – Not likely to cause offense or disagreement and somewhat dull; (n). – a pain killing drug or medicine.

Anoint* (v). – Put oil or water on somebody's head as part of a religious ceremony.

Antagonist* (n). – A person who actively opposes or is hostile to someone or something; an adversary.

Antagonize* (v). – Make somebody angry or to annoy somebody.

Antecedent* (n). – A thing or an event that exists or comes before another, and may have influenced it.

Anthropomorphic (adj.). – Having human characteristics; relating to or characterized by anthropomorphism.

Anticline (n). – A ridge or fold of stratified rock in which the strata slope downwards from the crest.

Antics (n). – Foolish, outrageous or amusing behavior.

Antiquated (adj.). – Old fashioned and not suitable for the modern world.

Antoinette. (adj.). – Highly praiseworthy, priceless one.

Antonym* (n). – A word opposite in meaning to another (e.g. good and bad).

Apartheid*(n). – The former official government policy in South Africa of separating people of different races and making them live apart.

Apathy* (n). – The feeling of not being interested in or enthusiastic about anything.

Aphorism (n). – An observation which contains a general truth, a concise statement of a scientific principle typically by a classical author.

Aplomb (n). – Self – confidence or assurance, especially when in a demanding situation

Apnea (n). – A medical condition in which somebody stops breathing for a short time while asleep.

Apocalypse (adj.). – Disclosure or revelation of great knowledge.

Apocalypse (n). – The total destruction of the world, the end of the world, as described in the Bible.

Apocryphal (adj.) – (of a story or statement) of doubtful authenticity, although widely circulated as being true; of or belonging to the apocrypha.

Apojee* (n). – Astronomy – the point in the orbit of the moon or the satellite at which it is farthest from the earth; the highest point at the development of something; a climax or culmination.

Apotheosis (n). – The highest point in the development of something; a culmination or climax; the elevation of.

Appall* (v). – Shock somebody very much.

Apparatchik (n). – A member of a communist party apart; an official in a large organization.

Apparition (n). – A ghost or an image of a person who is dead.

Apportion* (v). – Divide something among people; give a share of something to somebody.

Apropos (preposition). – On the subject of something/ somebody..

Apt.* (adj.). – Appropriate or suitable in the circumstances; having a tendency to do something.

Arable (adj.). – (of land) Used or suitable for growing crops; (n). – Arable land or crops.

Arboretum*(n). – A botanical garden devoted to trees.

Arcane (adj.). – Mysterious or secret, understood by a few.

Arcane* (adj.) – Mysterious or secret; understanding by a few.

Archetypal (adj.). – Having all the qualities that make somebody/something a typical example of a particular kind of person or thing.

Aron (n). – Teaching, singing and is of Hebrew origin; mountaineer, or mount of strength.

Arraign (v). – Bring a person to court of law in order to formally accuse him/her of a crime.

Array*(v). – Display or arrange (things) in a particular way.

Arteriosclerosis (n). – The thickening of the walls of the arteries.

Articulation* (n). – The action or manner in which the parts come together at a joint; formulation, expression, wording, statement.

Artifact (n). – An object made by a human being, typically one of historical interest, something observed in a scientific investigation or experiment that is naturally present but occurs as a result of the preparative or investigative procedure.

Artificer (n). – A skilled mechanic in the armed forces; Archaic – A skilled craftsman or inventor.

Ascetic* (adj.). – Not allowing yourself physical pleasures, especially for religious reasons.

Asceticism (n). – Severe self – discipline and avoiding all forms of indulgence, typically for religious reasons.

Askance (adverb). – With an attitude or look of suspicion or disapproval; suspiciously.

Asphyxiate (v). – Kill (someone) by depriving them of air; die by being deprived of air.

Assiduity (n). – Constant or close attention to what is doing.

Assiduously (adverb). – With great care and perseverance.

Assize (n). – HISTORICAL – A court which formally sat at intervals in each country of England and wales to administer the civil and criminal law.

Assuage (v). – Make it less intense, satisfy an appetite or desire.

Astride* (adverb). – With a leg on each side of something; (preposition). – With a leg on each side of; extending across.

Astute (adj.). – Having or showing an ability to accurately assess situations or people and turn this to one's advantage.

Asunder (adverb). – Apart.

Atavisti (adj.). – Relating to or characterized by reversion to something ancient or ancestral

Atelier (n). – A workshop or studio, especially one used by an artist or designer.

Atonement (n). – Feeling sorry for wrongdoing, the act of atoning for sin or wrongdoing (especially appeasing a deity), expiation, propitiation.

Auandary* (n). – A state of perplexity or uncertainty over what to do in a difficult situation.

Audacity (n). – Behavior that risks being shocking; ugliness.

Augment* (v). – Increase the amount, value, size etc. of something.

Augur* (v). – (of an event or circumstance) Portend a good or bad outcome; (n). – (in ancient Rome) a religious official who observed natural signs, the behavior of birds, interpreting these as an indication of divine approval or disapproval of proposed action.

Austere* (adj.). – Very simple, without decoration; (used about a person) very strict and serious.

Austerity. (n). – Severity of manners or attitude, the quality of being strict and serious in appearance or manner.

Auteur (n). – A film director who influences their films so much that they rank as their own.

Autocracy* (n). – A country that is ruled by one person who has complete power, a system of government of a country in which one has complete power.

Avalanche (n). – A very large amount of snow that slides quickly down the side of a mountain.

Avarice (n). – Extreme greed for wealth or material gain.

Avaricious (adj.). – Greedy, tweedy.

Aversion* (n). – A strong feeling of not liking, a thing that you do not like.

Avert* (v). – Prevent something unpleasant, prevent.

Avid*.(adj.). – Having an eager desire for; having or showing a keen interest in or enthusiasm for something.

Avocation (n). – FORMAL – A hobby or minor occupation.

Avow (v). – Say firmly and publicly what your opinion is, what you think is true, etc.

Awry (adj.). – Away from the usual or expected course; amiss; out of normal or correct position.; askew.

Bacon* (n). – Cured or thin pieces of salted or smoked meat from the back or sides of a pig.

Badger (v). – An animal with black and white lines on its head that lives in holes in the ground and comes out at night.

Bait. (v). – Deliberately annoy or taunt (someone); put bait on (a hook) or in (a trap, net, or fishing area) to entice fish or animals.

Baleful (adj.). – Threatening harm, menacing; having a harmful or destructive effect.

Balk (v). – Hesitate or be unwilling to accept an idea or undertaking.

Bamboozle (v). – Cheat or fool.

Banal* (adj.). – So lacking in originality as to be obvious and boring.

Banded* (adj.). – Marked with a stripe or stripes of a different color.

Banter (n). – Playful and friendly teasing remarks; (v). – Exchange remarks in a good humoured teasing way.

Baptism* (n). – The Christian religious rite of sprinkling water on a person's forehead or immersing them in water, symbolizing purification, or regeneration and admission to the church.

Bard* (n). – A person who writes poems; a poet.

Barge*. (n). – A long flat bottomed boat for carrying freight on canals and rivers, either by its own power or towed by another.

Barrage* (n). – A concentrated artillery bombardment over a wide area.

Batter* (v). – Hit somebody/something hard, many times, banging, fighting, scrap.

Beacon* (n). – A fire or light on a hill of a tower, often near the coast, which is used as a signal.

Beatific (adj.). – Feeling or expressing blissful happiness; Christian Theology – imparting holy bliss.

Bedazzled (v). – Greatly impress (someone) with outstanding ability or striking appearance; decorate or personalize (v). – (clothing or accessories) using sequins, beads, glitter, etc.

Bedeck* (v) – Decorate.

Bedevil*(v). – (of something bad) Cause great and continual trouble, torment or harassment.

Bedrock (n). – Solid rock underlying loose deposits such as soil or alluvium; the fundamental principles on which something is based.

Befog* (v). – Get confused.

Beget* (v). – Cause; bring about; (especially) of a man bring (a child) into existence by the process of reproduction.

Begrudgingly (adverb). – Reluctantly or resentfully

Beguile (v). – Charm or enchant (someone), often in a deceptive way; help (time) pass pleasantly.

Behemoth(n). – A huge or monstrous creature; something enormous, especially a large and a powerful organization.

Belch (v). – Emit wind noisily from the stomach through the mouth; (especially of a chimney) send out a large amount of smoke or flame).

Beleaguered (adj.). – In a very different situation, (of a place) surrounded by armed forces aiming to capture it or force surrender.

Bellicose (adj.). – demonstrating aggression and willingness to fight.

Belligerent* (n). – Aggressive.

Bellow* (v). – Shout in a loud deep voice, especially because you are angry; make a deep low sound, like a bull.

Benediction* (n). – A prayer asking for divine blessing, the utterance of a blessing, especially at the end of a religious service.

Benevolence* (n). – Kindness, vastness.

Bequeath (v). – Leave (property) to a person or other beneficiary by a will.

Berate* (v). – scold/criticize angrily.

Bereft* (adj.). – Completely lacking something; having lost something.

Beseech* (v). – To ask somebody for something in a worried way because you want or need it very much.

Besiege* (v). – Surround a place with an army.

Besprinkle* (v). – sprinkle all over with small drops or amounts of a substance.

Bestial* (adj.). – Of or like an animal or animals.

Bete noire (n). – A person or thing that one particularly dislikes.

Betrothed* (n). – The person to whom one is engaged.

Bewitch* (v). – Attract and interest somebody very much.

Bicameral* (adj.). – Consisting of two chambers.

Bier* (n). – A movable frame on which a coffin is placed before burial or cremation on which they are carried to the grave.

Bigamous* (n). – The crime of marrying someone while still legally married to someone else, bigamy.

Bingo* (n). – A game in which players mark off numbers on cards as the numbers are drawn randomly by a caller, the winner being the first person to mark off all their numbers; a call by someone who wins a game of bingo; used to express satisfaction at a sudden positive event or outcome.

Bipartisan (adj.). – Involving the agreement of operation of two political parties that usually oppose each other's policies.

Bizarre (adj.). – Very strange or unusual.

Blandishment (n). – A flattering or pleasing statement or action used as a means of gently persuading someone to do something, coaxing.

Blase* (adj.). – Unimpressed with or indifferent to something because one has experienced or seen it so often before.

Blaze* (v). – A large and often dangerous fire; a very bright show of light or color.

Blight(v). – Have a severely detrimental effect on; (n). – A thing that spoils or damages something; a plant disease, typically one caused by fungi such as mildows, rust and smuts.

Blip (v). – Open (the throttle of a motor vehicle) momentarily; (of an electronic device) Make a very short, high pitched sound or succession of sounds; (n). – An unexpected, minor and typically temporary deviation from a general trend.

Blip*(n). – A light flashing on the screen of a piece of equipment, sometimes with a short high sound, a small problem that does not last long .

Blister* (n). – A small bubble on the skin filled with serum and caused by friction, burning, or other damage. "The best treatment of blisters caused by splashing of hot liquid is putting in ice cubes".

Blithering* (adj.). – Complete; utter (used to express annoyance or contempt).

Blitzkrieg (n). – An intense military campaign intended to bring about a swift victory, a short period characterized by an intense effort to do something or a large quantity of something arriving.

Bloat* (v). – make or become swollen with fluid or gas; (n). – A disease of livestock characterized by an accumulation of gas in the stomach.

Blooper (n). – Baseball – an embarrassing error; a weakly hit fly ball.

Blotted (adj.). – Swollen with fluid or gas.

Blurb* (v). – A short description of a book, following a fine line between tradition and innovation.

Blurt* (v). – Say (something) suddenly and without careful consideration.

Bob* (v). – Move quickly up and down; to make something do this.

Bode(v). – Be a portent of a particular outcome.

Bogeyman* (n). – An imaginary evil spirit or being used to frighten children.

Boisterous (adj.). – Noisy, energetic, and cheerful; (of weather or water) wild or stormy.

Bolster (v). – Support or encourage somebody/something; to make something stronger.

Bolster* (n). – A long thick pillow that is put under other pillows, (v). – support or encourage somebody/something to make something stronger.

Boomerang* (v). – (of a plan or action) Recoil on the originator.

Borough* (n). – A town or district which is an administrative unit.

Bot* (n). – A computer program that works automatically, especially one that searches for and finds information on the internet.

Botch (v). – Do something badly; to make a mess of something.

Botox (n). – A drug prepared from botulin used to treat muscular conditions to remove wounds and wrinkles.

Boudoir* (n). – A woman's bedroom or small private room.

Bouffant (adj.). – (of a person's hair) Styled to stand out from the head in a rounded shape; (n). – A bouffant hairstyle.

Bough* (n). – One of the main branches of a tree.

Bourgeois (adj.). – Motionless or middle – class.

Bragging* (n). – Excessively proud and boastful talks about one's achievements or possessions; (adj.). – Exhibiting or characterized by excessive pride or boastfulness.

Bravado (n). – A bold manner or a show of boldness intended to impress or intimidate.

Brawl* (v). – Fight or quarrel in a rough or noisy way, (n). – A rough or noisy fight or quarrel.

Brazen* (adj.). – Bold and without shame.

Bridle (n). – The leather straps that you put on a horse's head so that you can control it when you are riding on it.

Brigand (n). – A member of a gang that ambushes and robs people in forests and mountains.

Brindled* (adj.). – (especially of a domestic animal) brownish or tawny with streaks of other colors.

Bringer* (n). – A bringer of something is someone who brings or provides it.

Brinkmanship (n). – The art or practice of pursuing a dangerous policy to the limits of safety before stopping, especially in politics.

Bristle* (v). – Be covered with or abundant in; (of hair or fur) stand upright from the skin, typically as a sign of anger or fear (n). – Short stiff hair on an animal's skin or a man's face.

Bristling (adj.). – Aggressively brisk or tense; (especially of hair), short, stiff and spiky.

Brook*.(n). – A small flow of water.

Brusque.(adj.). – Abrupt or offhand in speech or manner.

Brute* (n). – A cruel, violent man; a large strong animal.

Brutish* (adj. . – Cruel and unpleasant.

Bubonic* (adj.). – Caused or characterized by swollen inflamed lymph nodes in the armpit or groin.

Buffeted*(n). – (especially of wind or wave) Strike repeatedly and violently; batter.

Buffoon* (n). – A ridiculous but amusing person; a clown.

Bulge*. (n). – Around lump that sticks out on something; (v). – stick out in a lump from something that is usually fat.

Bulwark (n). – A defensive wall; an extension of a ship's sides above the level of the deck.

Bumblebee* (n). – A large hairy bee that makes a loud noise as it flies.

Bumbling* (adj.). – Incompetent; acting in a confused or ineffectual way.

Burly (adj.). – (of a person) Large and strong; heavily built.

Burnish* (v). – Polish (something, especially metal) by rubbing; (n). – The shine on a highly polished surface.

Burp (v). – Noisily release air from the stomach through the mouth; belch; (n). A noise made by air released from the stomach through the mouth; a belch.

Bushel* (n). – A measure of capacity of 8 gallons or 36.4 liters used for corn, fruit, liquid etc. U.S. 35.2 liters.

Bust* (v). – Arrest somebody; break or damage something so that it cannot be used; to arrest somebody.

Buttress(n). – A structure of stone or brick built against a wall to strengthen or support it; a source of support and defense.

Buzzword* (n). – A word or a phrase, often an item of jargon, that is fashionable at a particular time or in a particular context.

Byword (n). – A person or thing cited as a notable and outstanding example or embodiment of something; a word or expression summarizing a thing's characteristics or a person's principles.

Byzantine (adj.). – Relating to Byzantium (now Istanbul), the Byzantine Empire, or the Eastern Orthodox Church; (of a system or situation) excessively complicated, and typically involving a great deal of administrative detail.

Cacophonous (adj.). – Involving or producing a harsh, discordant mixture of sounds.

Cacophony (n). – A harsh discordant mixture of sounds.

Cadmean (adj.). – Relating to, or characteristic of England or its inhabitants, institutions etc., belonging to, relating to etc.

Cahoots (n). – Working together or making plans together in secret, collusion, combination, conjunction, conspiracy.

Cajole (v). – Persuade a person to do something or give something by being very nice to him/her.

Calamine (n). – A pink powder consisting of zinc carbonate and ferric oxide, used to make a soothing lotion or ointment; calamine ore.

Calamitous* (adj.). – Involving calamity; catastrophic or disastrous.

Caldera(n). – A large volcanic crater, especially formed by a major eruption leading to the collapse of the mouth of the volcano.

Caliph (n). – The chief Muslim civil and religious ruler, regarded as the successor of Muhammad.

Callous*(adj.) – Showing or having an insensitive and cruel disregard for others.

Calumny (n). – A false statement made about somebody in order to damage their reputation.

Cameo (n). – A small character part in a play or film played by a distinguished actor or a celebrity; a piece of jewellery,

Candid (adj.). – Truthful and straightforward; frank.

Canine* (n). – a dog, (adj.). – Relating to or resembling a dog or dogs.

Canker (n). – A destructive fungal disease of apple and other trees that results in damage to the bark, an ulcerous condition or disease of a human or animal.

Cannabis (n). – A drug made from a plant (hemp) that some people smoke for pleasure, but which is considered illegal.

Canny (adj.). – Having or showing shrewdness and good judgment, especially in money or business matters.

Canto* (n). – ITALIAN – cantus – One of the sections into which certain long poems are divided.

Captivate* (v). – Attract and hold somebody's attention.

Caress (v). – Touch or stroke gently or lovingly; (n) – a gentle or loving touch.

Caricature* (n). – A picture, description, or imitation of a person in which certain striking characteristics are exaggerated in order to create a comic or grotesque effect.

Carrion (n). – The decaying flesh of dead animals.

Cartel* (n). – A group of separate companies that agree to increase profits by fixing prices and not competing with each other.

Cask* (n). – A large wooden container in which alcoholic drinks etc. are stored.

"Leaders of all political parties leave no stone unturned in castigating their opponents"

Castigate* (v). – Reprimand (someone) severely.

Castrate* (v). – Remove the testicles (a male animal or man); (n). – A man or an animal whose testicles have been removed.

Cataclysm (n). – Calamity, unhappy conclusion, accident, adversity, affliction.

Catastrophe* (n). – An Event that causes great disappointment/difficulty; a sudden disaster causing great suffering.

Catastrophic (adj.). – Involving or causing sudden great damage, or suffering, extremely unfortunate, or unsuccessful.

Catharsis (n). – The process of releasing, and thereby providing relief from, strong or repressed emotions.

Cauldron(n). – A large pot (kettle) for cooking or boiling over an open fire.

Causation* (n). – The relationship between cause and effect; casually, the action of causing something.

Cavalier (n). – A supporter of Charles I in the English civil war.

Cavalry*(n). – The part of the army that fought on horses in the past; the part of the modern army that uses heavily protected vehicles.

Caveat (n). – A warning or proviso of specific stipulations, conditions or limitations.

Celibate (adj.). – Not married and never having sexual relations, often because of religious beliefs.

Cerebral (adj.). – Of the cerebrum of the brain; PHONETICS – another term for retroflex.

Cerebrate(adj.). – intellectual, scholarly, academic, studious.

Certitude (n). – Absolute certainty or conviction that something is the case; something that someone firmly believes is true.

Cessation (n). – The stopping of something; a pause in something.

Cesspool* (n). – An underground container for the temporary storage of liquid waste and sewage; a disgusting or a corrupt place.

Chafe (v). – (with reference to a part of the body) Make or become sore by rubbing against something; rub (a part of the body) to restore warmth or sensation.

Chaff (n). – The husks of corn or other seed separated by winnowing or threshing, worthless things, rubbish.

Chagrin* (n). – A feeling of being disappointed, annoyed or humiliated.

Chaperone (v). – Looking after a young woman by an old woman to ensure her good behavior.

Charde* (n). – An absurd pretense intended to create a pleasant or respectable appearance.

Chary* (adj.). – Cautiously or suspiciously reluctant to do something.

Chasm(n). – A deep hole in the ground, a wide difference of feelings, interests etc. between two people or groups.

Chasten*(v). – (of a rebuke or misfortune) Have a restraining or moderating effect on.

Chastise* (v). – Formal – criticize somebody for doing something wrong; Old – Fashioned – punish somebody physically.

Chastiser (n). – One who inflicts punishment in return for an injury or offense.

Chattel (n). – LAW – An item of property other than freehold land, including tangible goods and leasehold interests, bondslave.

Chauvinist (n). – A person with a prejudiced belief in the superiority of his/her own kind.

Checkmate (v). – Defeat or frustrate totally, put into checkmate.

Chieftain*(n) – Leader of a tribe

Chime (v). – (of a bell or a clock) Make melodious ringing sounds, typically to indicate the time.

Chipping* (n). – A small fragment of stone, wood, or similar material.

Chisel* (v). – Cut or shape (something) with a chisel, INFORMAL – NORTH AMERICAN – cheat or swindle (someone) out of something.

Chiselled (adj.). – (of wood or stone) Shaped or cut with a chisel; (of a man's facial features) strongly and clearly defined.

Chivalrous* (adj.). – Related to good behavior towards women; gallant, equidistant, benevolent, courteous.

Chokehold*(n). – A tight grip round a person's neck, used to restrain them by restricting their beating.

Choppy (adj.) – (of a sea, lake or river) Having many small waves; having a disjointed or jerky quality.

Chuckle (v). – Laugh quietly, giggle, gesture.

Chugging* (n). – The action or practice of approaching passersby in the street to ask for subscription or donation for a particular charity.

Churlish (adj.). – Rude in a mean – spirited and surly way.

Chutzpah (n). – Extreme self confidence or audacity.

Cinder (n). – A small piece of burning coal, wood etc.

Circumambulate (v). – FORMAL – Walk all the way round (something), cover, drift, encompass float, roam, ramble, stroll, trek, explore.

Circumnavigate (v). – Sail, fly or travel all around something, especially all the way around the world.

Circumvent (v). – Find a clever way of avoiding a difficulty or rule.

Citadel* (n). – FIGURATIVE – (in past times) a castle on high ground in or near a city where

Clairvoyance (n). – The supposed faculty of perceiving things or events in the future or beyond normal sensory contact.

Clamber (v). – Climb or move in an awkward and laborious way, typically both hands and feet; (n). – An awkward and laborious climb or movement.

Clamor (n). – A loud and confused noise, especially that of people shouting; (v). – (of a group of people) Shout loudly and insistently.

Clamor (v). – (of a group of people) Shout loudly and insistently; (n). A loud and confused noise, especially that of people shouting.

Clampdown* (n). – strong action to stop or control something.

Clandestine* (adj.) – Secret and often not legal.

Clang* (v). – Make a loud sound like that of a metal being hit.

Clank (v). – Make a loud unpleasant sound like pieces of metal hitting each other.

Clarion (n). – Historical – A shrill narrow – tube war trumpet. (adj.). – Loud and clear.

Clasp (v). – Hold somebody/something tightly.

Claustrophobia (n). – Extreme or irrational fear of confined places.

Claw (v). – Scratch or tear something with the claw or the finger nails on each digit of the foot in birds, lizards, and some mammals.

Cleft* (n). – A natural opening or crack; especially in a rock or in a person's chin.

Clergy*(n). – The body of all people ordained for religious duties, especially in the Christian church.

Cliche (n). – A phrase or idea that has been used so many times that it no longer has any real meaning or interest; platitude.

Clientele*(n). – All the customers, guests, or clients who regularly go to a particular shop, hotel, organization etc.

Clobber(v). – Hit (someone) hard; treat or deal with harshly; defeat heavily.

Cloister (n). – A covered passage with arches around a square garden, usually forming part of a large church (cathedral) or building people to live (monastery or convent).

Clotted butter.(n). – somewhere between butter and whipped cream with at least 35% butter.

Clouse (adj.). – A French policeman who always commits stupid mistakes.

Clover(n). – A herbaceous plant of the pea family with dense globular flower heads and leaves which are typically three – lobed. It is an important fodder and rotational crop.

Clunky (adj.). – Solid, heavy, and old – fashioned; making a clunking sound.

Clutch*(n). – The part of a vehicle etc., that you press with your foot when you are driving in order to change the gear; (v). – to hold something tightly when you are in pain, afraid or excited.

Clutter (v). – Cover or file (something) with an untidy collection of things; (n). – a collection of things lying about in an untidy manner.

Coalesce (v). – Come together to form one mass or whole.

Cockamamie (adj.). – Ridiculous; implausible.

Cocoon (n). – A covering of thin threads that some insects make to protect themselves before becoming adults.

Coddle (v). – Treat (someone) in an indulgent or overprotective way; cook (an egg) in water below boiling point, pamper.

Coercion*(n). – The practice of persuading someone to do something by using force or threat.

Cogent* (adj.). – Strongly and clearly expressed in a way that influences what people believe.

Cognition* (n). – The process by which knowledge and understanding is developed in the mind.

Cognoscenti (n). – People who are especially well informed about a particular subject.

Cohabit* (v). – FORMAL – (used about a couple) Live together as if they are married.

Coherent* (adj.). – (ideas, thoughts etc.) Clear and easy to understand; logical.

Coiffure (n). – A person's hairstyle.

Coistered (adj.). – Enclosed by or having a cloister; kept away from the outside world; shattered.

Coliseum (n). – A large theater, cinema, or stadium.

Colloquial(adj.). – (of language) Used in ordinary or familiar conversation; not formal or literacy.

Colloquialism (n). – A word or phrase that is not formal or literary and is used in ordinary or formal conversation.

Colloquy (n). – Formal – A conversation, a gathering for Discussion of theological questions.

Colossus (n). – A statue that is much bigger than life size, a person or thing of enormous size.

Comatose* (adj.). – Relating to or in a state of coma; extremely lethargic and sleepy.

Combatant (n). – A person who takes part in fighting, especially in war.

Combative*.(adj.). – Ready or eager to fight or argue.

Comorbidity (n). – More than one illness or disease occurring in one person at the same time.

Compatibility* (n). – A state in which two things are able to exist or occur together without any problem or conflict; a feeling of sympathy and friendship; computing the ability of one computer, a piece of software etc. to work with another.

Compatriot* (n). – A person coming from the same country as you.

Complacent* (adj.). – Feeling too satisfied with yourself or with a situation, so that you think that there is no need to worry.

Complexion (n). – The natural color, texture, and appearance of a person's skin.

Complicit* (adj.). – Involve others in an activity that is unlawful and morally wrong.

Composure* (n). – The state or feeling of being calm and in control of oneself.

Compunction (n). – A feeling of guilt or moral scruple that prevents or follows the doing of something bad; unease, caboose

Conceit* (n). – Too much pride in yourself and your abilities and importance. "It is always better to be gentle and sober in behavior with others rather than being a conceit."

Conceit* (n). – Unique comparisons and to describe unlikely situations; favorable opinion especially, excessive appreciation of one's own worth or virtue. The landlord's conceit of his own superior knowledge

Concertation* (n) – (especially in European politics) Cooperation, as among opposing factions, aimed at affecting a unified proposal or concerted action.

Conch* shell (n). – The shell of a sea creature. "Sea beaches of oceans are infested with conch shells, generating the source of income for residents".

Concoct* (v). – Make (a dish or meal) by combining various ingredients; create or devise (a story or plan).

Concoction (n). – Mixture, blend.

Concord* (n). – Agreement or harmony between people or groups.

Concourse (adj.). – A large open area inside or in front of a public building.

Condescension (n). – Patronizing attitude or behavior.

Confabulate* (v). – Formal – Engage in conversation; talk; Psychiatry – Fabricate imaginary experiences as compensation for loss of memory.

Conflagration* (n). – An extensive fire which destroys a great deal of land or property; blaze.

Conflate (v). – Combine (two or more, texts, ideas, sets of information) into one.

Confluence* (n). – The place where two or more rivers or areas of water join together to become one single river; Formal – The way in which two or more things come together to become one single thing.

Confound*(v). – Mix up with something else; cause surprise or confusion in (someone), especially by not according to their expectations.

Conglomerate. (n). – A large group of diversified businesses; groups and collections of things.

Conjecture* (v). – Guess about something without real proof or evidence.

Conjoin (v). – Join; combine.

Conjointly (adverb). – United, related to, made up of, or carried on by two or more in combination.

Conjugal (adj.). – connected with marriage and the relationship between husband and wife.

Conjure*(v). – (a spirit or ghost) Appear by means of a magical ritual; implore (someone) to do something.

Conjuring(n). – The performance of tricks which are seemingly magical, typically sleight of hand.

Connoisseur (n). – A person who knows a lot about art, good food, music etc.

Connotation* (n). – an idea expressed by a word in addition to its main meaning.

Consecrate (v). – State formally in a special ceremony that a place or an object can be used for religious purposes.

Consensual*(adj.). – Relating to or involving consent or consensus.

Conservatism*(n). – Commitment to traditional values and ideas with opposition to change or innovation; the holding of political views that favor free enterprise, private ownership, and socially traditional ideas.

Consociationalism (adj.). – A form of democratic power sharing.

Consortium*(n). – An association, typically of several companies; law–the right of association and companionship with one's husband or wife.

Conspicuous* (adj.). – Clearly visible; attracting notice or attention.

Constellation (n). – A group of stars forming a recognizable pattern of group of association or similar people or things.

Consternation (n). – A feeling of anxiety or dismay, typically at something unexpected.

constrain* (v) – compel or force someone to follow a particular course of action

Constrict*.(v). – Make narrower, especially by encircling pressure.

Constriction* (adj). – Obstruction, tightening, narrowing; (n). – The act of constricting, the state of being constricted.

Contagion (n). – The communication of disease from one person or organism to another by close contact, the spreading harmful ideas or practice.

Contagious* (adj.). – Capable of being transmitted by bodily contact with an infected person, deal with it.

Contemporaneous* (adj.) – Existing at or occurring at the same period of time.

Contentious* (adj.). – Likely to cause an argument.

Contiguous(adj.). – Showing a common border; touching; next or together in sequence.

Contort* (v). – Twist or bend out of the normal state.

Contortionist (n). – An entertainer who twists and bends their body into strange and unnatural positions.

Contrition (n). – The state of feeling remorseful and penitent.

Contrivance (n). – A device, especially in literary or artistic composition, which gives a sense of artificiality, the use of skill to create or bring about something, especially with a consequent effect of artificiality.

Contrive*(v). – Manage to do something, although there are difficulties; to plan or invent something in a clever/or dishonest way.

Conundrum (n). – A confusing and difficult problem or question, a question asked for amusement, typically with a pun in its answer; riddle.

Convivial (adj.). – (of an atmosphere or event) Friendly, lively, and enjoyable, jovial.

Coordinate (n). – One of the two sets of numbers and/or letters that are used to find the position of a point of an area on a map, graph etc.

Cordon*. (n). A line of circle of police, soldiers, or guards preventing access to or from an area or building.

Coronation* (n). – The ceremony of crowning a sovereign or a sovereign's consort.

Corpus callosum* (n). – A broad band of nerve fibers joining the two hemispheres of the brain.

Corral (v). – Gather together and confine a group of people or things) ; NORTH AMERICAN – Put or keep (livestock) in a corral.

Corroborate* (v). – Support a statement, idea, etc, by providing new evidence.

Cosmogonic (adj.). – A theory of the origin of the universe; the creation or origin of the world or universe.

Cosmogony (n). – A theory regarding the origin of the universe; the branch of science that deals with the origin of the Universe, especially the solar system.

Cosset (v). – Care and protect in an overindulgent way.

Coterie (n). – People with common interests who do things together in a small group and do not like to include others.

Couch (v). – Express a thought, idea etc. in a way mentioned, encrypt.

Countenance (n). – A person's face or his/her expression.

Covert (adj.). – Done secretly.

Covetousness (adj.). – The feeling of having a strong desire for the things that other people have.

Coyly. (adverb). – In a way that is or pretends to be shy, or like a child; in a shy or modest manner.

Cradle* (n). – A small bed for a baby and can often be moved from side to side.

Crassness (n). – Behavior that is stupid and does not consider how other people might feel.

Creak* (v). – Make the noise of wood bending or of something not moving smoothly.

Credulity (n). – A tendency to be too ready to believe that something is real or true.

Crescendo (v). – Increase in loudness or intensity; (n). – A noise or piece of music that gets louder and louder.

Crest (n). – The top of a mountain or hill; a comb or tuft of feathers, or fur, or skin on the head of a bird or other animal.

Crestfallen* (adj.). – Sad or disappointed.

Cretaceous (adj.). – Relating to or denoting the last period of the Mesozoic era, between the Jurrassic and Tertiary periods.

Cretin (n). – Congenial offense – a stupid person (used as a general term of abuse); DATED. MEDICINE – A person who is physically deformed and has learning difficulties because of congenital thyroid deficiency.

Crib* (v). – Copy illicitly or without acknowledgement.

Cringe. (v). – Feel disgusted or embarrassed, move away from something or somebody because you are frightened.

Crinkle* (v) – To have, or to make something have, thin folds or lines in it.

Cripple* (v). – Cause severe and disabling damage to; deprive of the ability to function normally.

Crippling*(adj.). – Causing a person to become unable to walk or move properly; causing a severe and insuperable problem.

Critique* (v). – Evaluate(a theory or practice) in a detailed and analytical way.

Crochet (n). – A handicraft in which yarn is made up into a textured fabric by means of a hooked needle; (v). – Make (a garment or piece of fabric) using crochet.

Crony*(n). – A close friend or companion.

Cronyism (n). – The appointment of friends and associates to positions of authority, without proper regard to their qualifications.

Crouch* (v). – Adopt a position where the knees are bent and the upper body and the upper body is brought forward and down, typically in order to avoid detection or to defend oneself.

Crumb* (n). – A very small piece of bread, cake, or biscuit.

Crumble* (v). – Break or make something break into very small pieces, disintegrate.

Crunch* (v). – Make a loud noise when you are eating something hard; make a loud noise like the sound of something being crushed.

Crusade* (n)). – A fight for something that you believe to be good or against something that you believe to be bad.

Crusader* (n). – Campaigner, coroner.

Cryogenic* (adj.) – Related to the freezing of dead human bodies at very low temperature, related to or involving the branch of physics that deals with the production and effects of very low temperatures – "a powerful cryogenic engine"

Cudgel (n). – A short, thick stick used as a weapon; (v). Beat very hot, burning, with a cudgel.

Culinary (adj.). – Connected with cooking.

Cull (v). – Reduce the population of (a wild animal) by selective slaughter: select from a large quantity; obtain from a variety of sources; (n). – A selective slaughter of animals.

Culling* (n). – Reduction of a wild animal population by selective slaughter.

Cupid (n). – Roman God of attraction and affection, erotic love; the God of desire.

Cuppa* (n). – A cup of tea.

Curmudgeon (n) – A bad – tempered person, especially an old one.

Cusp* (n). – A point of transition between two different states; a pointed end where two curves meet.

Cussedness (n). – Deliberate and stubborn unruliness and resistance to guidance and discipline.

Cymbal (n). – One of a pair of round metal plates used as musical instruments. Cymbals make a loud ringing sound when you hit them together or with a stick.

Cynic* (n). – A person who believes that people only do things for themselves, rather than to help others.

Cynical (adj.). – Concerned only with one's own interested and typically disregarding accepted standards in order to achieve them; believing that people are motivated purely by self interest, distrustful of human sincerity or integrity.

Cynically* (adverb). – Pessimistic and misanthropic, deeply distrustful.

Cynosure* (n). – A person or thing that is the center of attention or admiration.

Dabble* (v). – Become involved in something that is not very serious; put your hands, feet, etc. in water and move them around.

Dainty(adj.). – Delicately small and pretty, fastidious, especially concerning food).

Damnedest* (adj.). – INFORMAL AMERICAN – Used to emphasize the surprising nature of something.

Damsel* (n). – Archaic – Literary – a young unmarried woman.

Dang* (v). – Used in various expressions for emphasis to express anger or frustration; (adj.). – Used to emphasize something, especially to express anger or frustration.

Dangle (v). – Hang freely; to hold something so that it hangs down.

Dangling* (adj.) – Hanging or swinging loosely.

Dart* (n). – An object like a small arrow. It is thrown in a game or shot as a Weapon

Dastardly (adj.). – Wicked and cruel.

De – stress* (v). – Relaxing after going through a period of stress or hard work; reduce the amount of stress experienced.

Deacon (n). – (in Catholic, Anglican and orthodox churches) An ordained minister of an order ranking below that of priest.

Deadpanned (adj.). – Impassive or expressionless; (v) – Say something amusing while affecting a serious manner.

Debilitate* (v). – Make (someone) very weak and infirm; hinder, delay, or weaken.

Debilitating (adj.). – (of a disease or condition) Making someone very weak and infirm; tending to weaken something.

Debilitating (adj.). – Tending to weaken something; (of a disease or condition) Making someone very weak and infirm.

Debility (n). – Physical weakness, especially as a result of illness.

Debris* (n). – Pieces from something that has been destroyed, especially in an accident.

Debunk (v). – Expose the falseness or hollowness of (an idea or belief); reduce the inflated reputation of someone.

Decadent (adj.). – Corrupt, self – indulgent, dissipated.

Decapitate (v.). – Cut off a person's head.

Deciduous (adj.). – (used about a tree) Of a type that loses its leaves every autumn, temporary, transitory, fugacious, tending to disappear.

Decimate* (v) – Kill large numbers of people, animals or plants in a particular area.

Decleor (n). – SPANISH – Peculiar beyond or deviating from the usual or expected, wind deflector.

Declutter (v). – Remove unnecessary items from (an untidy or overcrowded place).

Decrepit* (adj.). – Worn out or ruined because of age or neglect; (of a person) elderly and infirm.

Decrepit* (adj.). – worn out impaired.

Decrepitude* (n). – Feebleness, infirmity, weakness, frailty, sickliness, old age, senility; the state of being decrepit.

Decryption (n). – The process of transferring data that has been rendered unreadable through encryption back to its unencrypted form.

Deferential (adj.). – Showing respect, deference.

Defile* (v). – Damage the purity or appearance of; mar or spoil; desecrate or profane (something sacred).

Defrock (v). – Deprive (someone) of professional status or membership of a prestigious group.

Deft* (adj.). – Neatly skillful and quick in one's movements demonstrating skill and cleverness.

Deftly* (adverb). – In a way that is neatly skillful and quick in movement, in a clear way

Delegitimize* (v). – Withdraw legitimate status or authority from.

Delirium. (n). – A mental state where somebody becomes delirious, confused due to high fever, lucidity, anxiety, disorientation.

Delude* (v). – Make somebody believe something that is not true.

Deluge* (n). – A severe flood.

Delusion* (n). – Mitigation, misapprehension; an idiosyncratic belief or impression maintained despite being contradicted by reality or rational argument, typically as a symptom of mental disorder.

Delve* (v). – Reach inside a receptacle and search for something; ARCHAIC – dig; excavate.

Demeanor* (n). – Outward behavior or meaning; conduct; bearing, appearance.

Demonize* (v). – Portray as wicked and threatening.

Denizen (n). – A person, animal, or plant that lives or is found in a particular place.

Denouement (n). – The outcome of a situation, when something is decided or made clear; the final part of a play, film, or narrative in which the strands of the plot are drawn together and matters are explained or resolved.

Depraved* (adj.). – Morally bad, corrupt, cognate.

Deprecate* (v). – Express disapproval of; another term for depreciate.

Deprecated (v). – Express disapproval of; discourage or belittle (something).

Deprecatory (adj.). – Expressing disapproval; disapproving.

Depredation* (n). – acts that cause severe damage or destruction to property, lives etc.

Derelict* (adj.). – In a very poor condition as a result of disuse and neglect.

Deride (v). – Express contempt for; ridicule.

Derision(n). – Contemptuous ridicule or mockery.

Derision* (n). – Contemptuous ridicule or mockery; actions or statements showing that you think someone or something ridicule or of no value.

Derisive (adj.). – Expressing contempt or ridicule.

Derisory (adj.). – Too small or of little value to be considered seriously.

Desecrate* (v). – Damage a place of religious importance or treat it without disrespect. “All religious places are abodes of super souls. None can think of desecrating them”

Desiccation* (n). – The process of becoming completely dry.

Desolate* (adj.). – (used about a place) Empty in a way that seems very sad, (used about a person) lonely, very unhappy and without hope.

Desolation* (n). – A state of complete emptiness or destruction, great unhappiness or loneliness.

Despise (v). – Feel contempt or a deep repugnance for.

Despoil (v). – Steal or violently remove valuable possessions from; plunder

Despondency* (n). – Pleasure delivered by someone from another person's misfortune.

Despot* (n). – A ruler with great power, especially one who uses it in a crucial way.

Despotism (n). – A country or political system where the ruler holds absolute power; the exercise of absolute power, especially in a cruel and oppressive way.

Destitute* (adj.). – Without any money, food or a home.

Desultory (adj.). – Lacking a plan, purpose or enthusiasm, casual, half – hearted; (of conversation or speech) going from one subject to another in a half hearted way; occurring randomly or occasionally.

Detour* (v). – take a long or roundabout route; (n). – a long or roundabout route that is taken to avoid something.

Detritus (n). – Waste or debris of any kind, gravel, sand, salt or other material produced by erosion, organic matter produced by decomposition of organisms.

Devastate* (v). – Destroy or ruin; cause (someone) severe and overwhelming shock or grief.

Deviant (adj.). – Departing from usual or accepted standards, especially in social or sexual behavior; (n). – A deviant person or thing.

Devious. (adj.). – Clever, deceitful or dishonest, not straightforward.

Devour* (v). – Eat hungrily or quickly; read quickly or eagerly; (of fire or a similar force) destroy completely.

Devout*(adj.). – Very religious.

Devoutly* (adverb). – In a manner that shows deep religious feeling or commitment; in a totally committed and sincere way.

Dexterity (n). – Skill at doing things, especially with your hands.

Dexterous (adj.). – Showing or having skill, especially with the hands, deft, adroit.

Diabolical (adj.). – Disgracefully bad or unpleasant

Dialectic* (n). – The art of investigating the truth of opinions.

Dialectical* (adj.). – Relating to the logical discussion of ideas and opinions; concerned with or acting through opposing forces.

Diaspora* (n). – A scattered population whose origin lies in a separate geographic locale.

Diatribe (n). – A forceful and bitter attack against someone.

Dichotomy* (n). – A division or contrast between two things that are or are represented as being opposed or entirely different; Botany – repeated branching in two parts.

Didactic (adj.). – Designed to teach people something, especially a moral lesson; telling people things rather than letting them find out for themselves.

Diffidence (n). – Modesty or shyness resulting from a lack of confidence.

Digress (v). – Leave the main subject temporarily in speech or writing.

Dilapidated* (adj.). – (used about buildings, furniture, etc.) Old and broken, tumbledown.

Dilatory (adj.). – Slow to act; intended to cause delay.

Diminution (n). – Of reduction in the size, extent, or importance of something; MUSIC – Shortening the time values of notes in a melodic part.

Diminutive (adj.). – Extremely or unusually small; (n). – A diminutive word or suffix.

Dingy (adj.) – Dirty and dark.

Discern*(v). – Recognize or find out.

Discernible* (adj.) – Observable, apparent, obvious, direct, noticeable.

Discomfiture* (n). – A feeling of unease or embarrassment; awkwardness.

Discordant* (adj.). – That spoils a general feeling of agreement.

Discreet (adj.). – Careful and prudent in one's speech or actions, especially in order to keep something confidential or to avoid embarrassment.

Disdain* (n). – the feeling that sb/sth is not good enough to be respected.

Disdainful (adj.). – Showing contempt or lack of respect.

Disembowel* (v). – Cut open and remove the internal organs of.

Disenfranchise (v). – Deprive (someone) of the right to vote, deprive (someone) of right or privilege; Archaic – deprive (someone) of the rights and privileges of a free inhabitant of a borough, city or country.

Dishevel* (v). – Make (a person's hair or clothes) untidy. Into long locks.

Disingenuous (adj.). – Not candid or sincere, typically by pretending that one knows less about something than one really does.

Disparage* (v). – Talk about somebody/something in a critical way; say that somebody/something is of little value or importance.

Disparaging (adj.). – Expressing the opinion that something is of little worth; derogatory.

Disparate* (adj.). – Consisting of people or things that are very different from each other in character and quality.

Dispassionate (adj.). – Not influenced by strong emotions, and so able to be rational and impartial.

Dispensation*(n). – Exemption from a rule or usual requirement.

Dissenter*(n). – A person who dissents.

Distraught (adj.). – Very worried and upset.

Dither* (v). – Be indecisive, add white noise to (a digital recording) reduce distortion of low – amplitude signals; (n). – Indecisive behavior.

Divvy (v). – Share out; (n). – A dividend or share, especially of profits earned by a co-operative.

Doctrine (n). – Belief or set of beliefs held and taught by a Church, political party, or other group.

Dodderer (adj.). – Golden age, old person, one who dodders from old age, senior citizen, an elderly person, feeble.

Dodgy* (adj.). – Dishonest or unreliable; of low quality; potentially dangerous.

Doe like (adj.). – Resembling or character of a doe (a female rabbit, deer or hare); submissively tender.

Doggedly (adverb). – In a persistent or tenacious manner.

Dollop (n). – INFORMAL – A lump of something soft, especially food.

Dominion* (n). – The power to rule and control; an area controlled by one government or ruler.

Don* (v). – Put on (an item of clothing).

Doodle* (v). – Draw or sketch aimlessly, especially when preoccupied; to kill time.

Doomsday* (n). – A time or event of crisis or great danger; the day of the last judgment; the last day of the world's existence.

Doughty* (adj.). – Brave and persistent.

Douse(v). – pour a liquid over, drench, and rain water on the ground.

Dowager* (n). – A dignified elderly woman; widow with a title or property derived from her late husband.

Doyen* (n). – The oldest, most respected, or most experienced member of a group or profession.

Doyenne (n). – The most respected or prominent woman in a particular field.

Draconian (adj.). – (of laws or their application) Excessively harsh.

Dreary* (adj.). – Depressingly dull and bleak or repetitive; dull.

Dribble (v). – (used about a liquid) Move downwards in a thin flow; Make liquid move in this way.

Drool* (v). – Let liquid (saliva) come out from the mouth, usually at the sight or smell of something to eat.

Droop (v). – Bend or hang downwards limply; cause to bend or hang downwards; sag down from or as if from weariness or dejection.

Drubbing (n). – A beating; a thrashing; informal – a resounding defeat in a match or contest.

Drudge (n). – Hard and boring work.

Duck (v). – Lower the head of the body quickly to avoid a blow of a missile or so as not to be seen; push or plunge (someone).

Dumbstruck* (adj.). – So shocked or surprised as to be unable to speak.

Dumfounded (adj.). – Very surprised.

Duopoly(n). – A situation in which two suppliers dominate the market for a commodity or service.

Dwarfish* (adj.). – Like a dwarf; being especially small or stunted.

Dwindle (v). – Become smaller or weaker

Dyspepsia* (n). – Indigestion, feeling of unusual fullness following needs; nausea, loss of appetite, heartburn.

Dystopia (n). – An imaginary place where everything is as bad as it can be. 862. flip*(v). – to turn (something) over with a quick movement; to throw something into the air and make it turn over.

Dystopian (adj.). – Relating to an imagined state or society where there is great suffering; (n). – a person who imagines or foresees a state or society with great suffering.

Eavesdrop (v). – Listen secretly to other people talking, overhear, snoop, pry.

Ebb* (v). – (of tide water) Move away from the land, recede.

Ebullient (adj.). – Cheerful and full of energy; ARCHAIC – (of liquid or matter) Boiling or agitating as if boiling.

Ecclesiastical (adj.). – Relating to the Christian Church or its clergy.

echelon(n). – A level of command, or rank in an organization, profession, or society; a formation of troops, ships etc. in parallel rows.

Eclectic* (n). – A person who derives ideas, style, or taste from a broad and diverse range of sources; (adj.). – Deriving ideas, style, or taste from a broad and diverse range of sources.

Edict* (n). – An official order or statement issued by somebody in a position of power.

Edifice (n). – A large imposing building, a complex system of belief.

Edifying*(adj.). – Providing moral or intellectual instructions; used to express one's disapproval of something.

edigree* (n). – The record of descent of an animal, showing it to be pure – breed; the recorded ancestry.

Eerie. (adj.) – Strange or frightening.

Effacement (n). – The thinning or obliteration of tissue or narrowing of an internal anatomical space.

Effeminate (adj.). – (used about a man or his behavior) Like a woman.

Effete* (adj.). – Affected and overly refined;(of a man) behaving in a way traditionally associated with women and regarded as inappropriate for a man, no longer of an effective action.

Effusive* (adj.). – Showing or expressing gratitude, pleasure, or approval in an unrestrained or heartfelt manner.

Egalitarian (adj.). – (used about a person, system, society etc.) Following the principle that everyone should have equal rights.

Egalitarian* (n). A person who advocates or supports the principle of equality for all; (adj.) – believing in the principle of equality.

Egregious (adj.). – Outstandingly bad or shocking.

Eke (v). – Manage to make a living with difficulty; make an amount or supply of something last longer by using or consuming it frugally.

Elicit (v). – Evoke or draw out (a reaction, answer, or fact) from someone, draw forth (something that is latent or potential) into existence.

Elide (v). – Omit (a sound or syllable) when speaking; merge, join together.

Ellation* (n). – Extreme happiness, euphoria, enthusiasm, bliss, ecstasy, excitement, exhilaration, glee, joyfulness.

Eloquence* (n). – Or performers. Fluent or persuasive speaking or writing.

Eloquent* (adj.). – Able to use language and express your opinions well, especially when you speak in public.

Elusive* (adj.). – Difficult to remember, find, catch, or achieve.

Emanation (n). – Something which originates or issues from a source, (in various mystical traditions) a being or force which is the Manifestation of God.

Emancipate (v). – Set free, especially from legal, social, or political restrictions; Law – set a child free from the authority of its parents.

Emasculate (v). – Make weaker or less effective, insecure

Emasculate*(v). – Deprive (a man) of his male role or identity.

Embellishment (n). – A decorative detail or feature added to something to make it more attractive.

Ember (n). – A piece of coal or wood that is not burning, but is still red and hot after the fire is extinguished.

Embolism (n). – Obstruction of an artery, typically by a clot of blood or an air bubble.

Embroil* (v). – Involve(someone) deeply in an argument, conflict, or difficult situation; bring into a state of confusion or disorder.

Embrosia* (n). – The food of the gods; a fungal product used as food by ambrosia.

Emigrate (v). – Leave one's location, such as one's native country or region, to live in another.

Emotive* (adj.). – Causing strong feelings.

Empanel*(v). – In a law court, to choose the people who will form the jury for a trial.

Empathize* (v). – Understand and share the feelings of another.

Empathy* (n). – The ability to understand and share the feeling of another.

Emulate* (v). – Try to do something as well as, or better than somebody.

Emulation (n). – Effort to match or surpass a person or achievement, typically by imitation.

Enamored (v). Be filled with love for, have a liking or admiration for.

Encapsulate (v). – Express the salient features of (something) succinctly; enclose (something) in or as if in a capsule. "Would you like to encapsulate your achievements after your retirement" ?

Encompass* (v). – Surround and have or hold within; Archaic – cause to take place.

Encryption*(n). – The process of converting information or data into a code, especially to prevent unauthorized access.

Enervate* (v). – Make (someone) feel drained of energy or vitality; Literary – lacking in energy or vitality.

Enervating* (adj.). – Causing one to feel drained of energy or vitality.

Enfeebled* (adj.). – Made weak or feeble.

Enigma (n). – A person, thing or situation that is difficult to understand.

Enigmatic* (adj.). – Mysterious, insidious, ambiguous, obscure, vague.

Enormity* (n). – Seriousness, largeness of size.

Enrapture* (v). – Give intense pleasure or joy to.

Ensconce (v). – Establish or settle (someone) in a comfortable, safe place.

Ensemble (n). – A group of items viewed as a whole rather than individually; a group of musicians, actors, or dancers, who perform together.

Entangle*(v). – Cause to become twisted together with or caught in.

Enticing* (adj.). – Attractive and interesting.

Entrench*(v). – Dig or occupy a trench for defence.

Entrenched* (adj.). – (of an attitude, habit or belief) firmly established and difficult or unlikely to change; ingrained.

Ephemeral (adj.). – Lasting or used for only a short period of time.

Epicurean (n). – A disciple or student of the Greek philosopher Epicurus; a person devoted to sensual enjoyment especially that derived fine food and drink.

Epiphany (n). – The manifestation of Christ to the Gentiles as represented by the Magie (2:1 – 12) ; A moment of sudden and great revelation or realization.

Epitomize(v). – Be a perfect example of, give a summary of a written book.

Epitomize*(v). – Be a perfect example of; give a summary.

Epochat (n). – A period of time in history (that is important because of special events, characteristics etc.)

Eponymous (adj). – (of a person) Giving their name to something; (of a thing) named after a person or a group.

Equestrian (adj.). – FORMAL – Connected with horse riding.

Ergonomically (adverb). – Human engineering, human factors engineering.

Errand (n). – A job that you do, often for someone else that involves going somewhere to buy something, deliver goods.

Erudite (adj. – FORMAL – Having or showing great knowledge that is based on careful study.

Erudite (adj.). – Having or showing great knowledge or learning.

Erudition (n). – Reportage, knowledge.

Ervid (adj.). – Intensely enthusiastic or passionate.

Eschatology (n). – The part of theology concerned with death, judgment, and the final destiny of the soul and of humankind.

Eschew* (v). – Deliberately avoid using; abstain from.

Escrow (n). – A bond, deed, or other document kept in the custody of a third party; (v). – Place in custody or trust until a specified condition has been fulfilled.

Esoteric (adj.). – FORMAl – Intended for or likely to be understood or enjoyed by only a few people with a special knowledge or interest.

Esoteric* (adj.). – Intended for or likely to be understood or enjoyed by only few people with a special knowledge or interest.

especially as a result of poverty or neglect.

Espiocrat (n). – A professional spy, a member of an espionage bureaucracy. "Would you like to be an espiocrat for your country ?"

Espouse*(v). – Adopt or support (a cause, belief or a way of life).

Etch* (v). – (of an acid or other solvent) Corrodes or eats away the surface of (something).

Ethereal* (adj.). – FORMAL – Extremely delicate and light, in a way that seems unreal; of heaven or the spirit, airy, pneumatic.

Ethnic* (adj.). – Relative to a population sub – group with a common national/cultural tradition.

Etiquette*.(n). – The rules of polite and correct behavior.

Eucharist (n). – The Christian service, ceremony, or sacrament commemorating the last supper in which bread and wine are consecrated and consumed.

Eulogist (n). – A person who gives a speech or piece of writing that says good things about somebody/something. "Your positive thinking about people around you, makes you a great eulogist".

Eulogize (v). – Praise somebody/something very highly.

Euphemism (n). – A mild or direct word of expression substituted for one considered to be too harsh or blunt when referring to something unpleasant or embarrassing.

Euphemistic (adj.). – Polite; substitute; using or of the nature of euphemism.

Euphoria (n). – A feeling or state of immense excitement and happiness.

Euphoric (adj.) – Characterized by or feeling intense excitement and happiness.

Evangelism (n). – Zealous advocacy or support of a particular support.

Evangelist (n). – A person who seeks to convert others to the Christian faith, especially by public preaching; the writer of the four gospels (Mathew, Mark, Luke or John).

Eviscerate (v). – Deprive (something) of its essential content; disembowel (a person or animal). SURGERY – Remove the contents of (the eyeball).

Evocative (adj.). – Bringing strong images, or feelings to mind.

Exactitude (n). – The quality of being exact; precision; accuracy.

Exasperate*(v). – Irritate and frustrate someone intentionally.

Exasperation (n). – A feeling of intense irritation or annoyance.

Excrescence (n). – A distinct outgrowth on a body or plant, resulting from disease or abnormality, an unattractive or superfluous object or feature.

Excruciating (adj.). – Extremely painful.

Exfiltrate (v). – Withdraw (troops or spies) surreptitiously, especially from a dangerous situation.

Exhort* (v). – Strongly encourage or urge (someone) to do something.

Existential* (adj.). – Relating to existence, affirming or implying the existence of something.

Exorcize (v). – Make an evil spirit leave a place by special prayers/to remove something painful from mind.

Expediency* (n). – Advantage, benefit, profit, gain, mileage, facility, convenience, comfort, privilege.

Expedient (adj.). – (of an action) Convenient and practical although possibly improper or immoral; (n). – A means of attaining an end, especially one that is convenient but possibly improper and immoral.

Expiate (v). – Make amends or reparation for (guilt or wrongdoing).

Expletive* (n). – a rude word spoken in anger.

Explicit* (n). – Clear; making something easy to understand.

Expound*(v). – Present and explain (a theory or idea) in detail; explain the meaning of (a literary or doctrinal work).

Exquisite*.(adj.). – Extremely beautiful and pleasing.

Extermination (n). – Killing, eradicating, uprooting, extirpating.

Extol* (v). – Praise enthusiastically.

Extraneous*.(adj.). – Irrelevant or unrelated to the subject being dealt with; of external origin.

Exuberant (adj.). – Full of energy, excitement and cheerfulness.

Exult* (v). – Feel or show triumphant elation or jubilation.

Factotum (n). – An employee who does all kinds of work.

Fad* (n). – Fashion/interest not lasting long.

Faience (n). – Glazed ceramic ware, in particular decorated tin – glazed earthenware of the type which includes delftware and maiolica.

Fallible* (adj.). – Able or likely to make mistakes.

Falter* (v). – (intransitive) – Become weaker or less effective.

Faltering (adj.). – Losing strength or momentum, speaking hesitatingly, moving unsteadily or unsteadily.

Fanaticism* (n). – An extreme and often unquestioning enthusiasm, devotion, or zeal for something, such as a religion, political stance, or cause.

Fang* (n). – The biting mouthpart of a spider, the tooth of a venomous snake, by which poison is ejected.

Farcical* (n). – Relating to or resembling farce, especially because of absurd or ridiculous aspects.

Fascism* (n). – Autocracy, bureaucracy.

Fastidious* (adj.). – Very concerned about matters of cleanliness; very attentive to and concerned about accuracy and detail.

Fatalism (n). – The belief that all events are predetermined and therefore inevitable; a submissive attitude to events, resulting from a fatalistic attitude.

Fealty (n). – A feudal tenant or vassal's sworn loyalty to lord; formal acknowledgment of loyalty to a lord.

Feckless (adj.). – Lacking initiative or strength of character; irresponsible.

Feigned (v). – Pretend to have a particular feeling or that you're tired or ill.

Ferocity* (n). – The state or quality of being ferocious or forgery.

Fervid*(adj.). – Intensely enthusiastic/passionate, especially to an excessive degree.

Fester(v). – (of a wound or sore) Become septic; suppurate; (of food or rubbish) become rotten and offensive to the senses.

Festoon* (n). – A chain of lights, colored papers, flowers etc. used to decorate something, especially as a part of a celebration; (v) – Decorate something with colored paper, flowers, lights, etc. often as a part of a celebration.

Fetish (n). – A form of sexual desire in which gratification is linked to an abnormal degree to a particular object, item of clothing, part of the body etc.

Fetter* (n). – A chain or manacle used to restrain a prisoner, typically placed around the ankles; (v). – restrain with chains or manacles, typically around the ankles.

Fickle* (adj.). – Always changing your mind or feelings so you cannot be trusted.

Fidelity (n). – (used about translations, the reproductive etc.) The quality of being accurate or close to the original; FORMAL – the quality of being faithful, especially to a wife or husband by not having sexual relationship with anyone else.

Fidgety (adj.). – Restless or uneasy; inclined to fidget.

Fiduciary. (adj.). – Involving trust between a trustee and beneficiary.

Fiefdom (n). – A territory or sphere of operation controlled by a particular person or group.

Fiend (n). – A very cruel person; a person who is very interested in one particular thing.

Fiery* (adj.). – Looking like fire, quick to become angry.

Fintech (n). – Computer program and other technology used to support or enable banking and financial services.

Fiscal* (adj.). – Related to government revenue, especially taxes.

Fissiparous (adj.). – Inclined to cause or undergo division into separate parts or groups.

Fissure*. (n). – A long, narrow opening or line of breakage made by cracking or splitting, especially in rock or earth.

Flabbergasted (adj.). – Extremely surprised and/or shocked.

Flagellation (n). – Flogging or beating, either as a religious discipline or for sexual gratification.

Flagship* (n). – The mainship in a fleet of ships in the navy; the most important product, service, building etc. that an organization owns.

Flak (n). – Strong criticism; anti aircraft fire.

Flamboyance* (n). – The quality of being very confident in your behavior and liking to be noticed by other people, for example because of the way you dress or talk.

Fledgling (n). – A young bird that has just fled, a person or organization that is immature, inexperienced or underdeveloped.

Fleeting (adj.). – Lasting for a very short time.

Fling* (v). – Throw somebody/something suddenly and carelessly or with great force.

Flippant (adj.). – Not showing a serious or respectful attitude.

Flirtatious (adj.). – Behaving in such a way as to suggest a playful sexual attraction to someone.

Flog* (v). – Hit somebody hard several times with a stick or a long thin piece of leather (whip) as a punishment.

Flounder* (v). – Struggle or stagger clumsily in mud or water; struggle mentally, show or feel great confusion.

Fluke* (n). – INFORMAL – A surprising and lucky result that happens by accident, not because you have been clever or skillful.

Flurry (n). – A small swirling mass of something, especially snow or leaves, moved by sudden gusts of wind.

Flutter (v). – Move or make something move quickly and lightly, especially through the air.

Foliage*(n). – All the leaves of a tree or a plant.

Folklore* (n). – Traditional stories and beliefs.

Foolhardy (adj.). – Recklessly bold or rash.

Forage (v). – Of a person or animal) search widely for food or provisions; (n). – Food such as grass or hay for horses and cattle; fodder; a wide search over an area in order to obtain something, especially food or provisions.

Foray (n). – A sudden attack or incursion into enemy territory, especially to obtain something; a raid.

Foreclosure (n). – Hinder; forehinder, outstandning (Swedish).

Forge* (v). – Make an illegal copy of something; put a lot of effort into making something strong and successful; (n). – A place where objects are made by heating and shaping metal.

Forlorn (adj.). – Pitifully sad and abandoned or lonely

Forlorn* (adj.). – Pitifully sad and abandoned or lonely; (of an aim or endeavor) unlikely to succeed or be fulfilled.

Fortitude* (n). – Courage and patience shown by somebody who is suffering great pain or facing great difficulties.

Fortuitous (adj.). – Happening by chance rather than intention, happening by a lucky chance; fortunate.

Frag (v). – Deliberately kill (an unpopular senior officer) with a hand grenade.

Frailty (adj.). – Weakness and lack of health and strength.

Frailty (n). – Weakness of a person's body or character.

Frailty* (n). – The condition of being weak and delicate; weakness in character or morals.

Fraught (adj.). – Causing or affected by anxiety or stress; (of a situation or course of action) Filled with or likely to result in (something undesirable).

Fraught (adj.). – Causing or affected by anxiety or stress; (of a situation or course of action) filled with or likely to result in (something undesirable).

Freak (n). – A very unusual and unexpected event or situation; a person, animal, or plant with an unusual physical abnormality.

Frenemy (n). – A person with whom one is friendly despite a fundamental dislike or rivalry.

Frenetic* (adj.). – Fast and energetic in a rather wild and uncontrolled way.

Frenzy*.(n). – A state or period of uncontrolled excitement.

Fresco (n). – A painting on a wall., ceiling etc. painted while the plaster is still not completely dry; the method of painting in this way.

Fret*. (v). – To be worried and unhappy about something; (n). – One of the bars across the long thin part of a guitar, etc. that show you where to put fingers to produce a particular sound.

Fringe* (n). – The part of your hair that is cut so that it hangs over your forehead, a border for decoration on a piece of clothing etc. that is made of lots of hanging threads.

Frisbee. (n). – A concave plastic disc designed for skimming through the air as an outdoor game or amusement.

Fritter (v). – Waste time, money or energy on trifling matters. Boomerang (n). – A curved flat piece of wood that can be thrown so that it will return to the thrower, traditionally used by Australian Aboriginal people as a hunting weapon.

Frivolous (adj.). – Not having any serious purpose or value; (of a person) carefree and superfluous.

Frivolous* (adj.). – Not serious; silly.

Frugal (adj.). – Economical, sparing and thrifty; careful in the use of one's money or resources.

Fudge (v). – Avoid giving clear and accurate information, answers, opinions etc.

Fuehrer* (n). – A tyrannical leader.

Fulminate (v). – Express vehement protest; LITERARY – explode violently or flash like lightning.

Fulmination*(n). – An expression of vehement protest, a violent explosion or a flash like lightning.

Fumble* (v). – Try to find or take hold of something with your hands in a nervous or careless way, mishandle, mismanage, spoil.

Furrow (v). – Make a rut, groove, or trail in (the ground or the surface of something).

Furtive (adj.). – Suggestive of guilty nervousness; attempting to avoid notice or attention, typically because of guilt or belief that discovery would lead to trouble; secretive.

Fusillade (n). – A series of shots fired or missiles thrown all at the same time or in quick succession.

Gag* (v). – To put a piece of cloth over or in a person's mouth to stop the person; to restrain by force or authority from freedom of speech; silence.

Gallant* (adj.). – (of a person or their behavior) Brave; heroic; (of a man) charmingly attentive and chivalrous to women.

Galore* (adj. – In abundance.

Gamut (n). – The complete range or scope of something; Music – a complete set of musical notes; the range of a voice or instrument.

Gasp*(v). – Catch one's breath with an open mouth, going to pain or astonishment.

Gean (n). – The wild or sweet cherry, which is native to both Eurasia and North America.

Generic* (adj.). – (used about a product, especially a drug) Not using the name of the company that made it, shared by, including or typical of a whole group of things; not specific.

Geriatric* (adj. – Relating to old people, especially with regard to their healthcare; (n). – An old person who is receiving special care.

Gerrymander (v). – Manipulate the boundaries (of an electoral constituency) so as to favour one party or class.

Gerund* (n) – A noun ending in '-----ing' that has been made from a verb.

Ghettoize (v). – Put in or restricted to an isolated or segregated place, group or situation.

Ghoul (n). – An evil spirit or phantom, especially one supposed to rob graves and feed on dead bodies.

Gig (n). – Informal, a single performance by a musician or group of musicians, especially playing modern or pop music.

Girdle (n). – A belt or cord worn around the waist, a woman's elasticated corset extending from waist to thigh; (v) – Encircle (the body) With a girdle; cut through the bark all the way round (a tree or branch), typically in order to kill it or to kill a branch to make the tree fruitful.

Gladiator (n). – (in ancient Rome) a man trained to fight with weapons against other men or wild animals in an arena.

Gleam* (n). – A soft; light that shines for a short time; a sudden expression of an emotion in somebody's eyes.

Glean (v). – Obtain information from different sources often with difficulty, gathering (leftover grain) after a harvest.

Gleeful (adj.). – Exuberantly or triumphantly.

Gleefully* (adverb). – Cheerfully, cheerily, delightedly, gaily, happily and excitedly.

Glib (adj.). – Using words in a way that is clever and quick but not sincere.

Glimmer* (v). – Shine faintly with a wavering light; (n). – A faint or wavering light; a faint sign of a feeling or quality, especially a desirable one.

Glisten (adj.). – (used about wet surfaces) To shine

Glitch* (n). – A sudden, usually temporary malfunction or fault of equipment; (v). – suffer a sudden malfunction or fault.

Glitz(v). – Make (something) glamorous or showy, (n). – extravagant but superficial display. Plethora*(adj.). – An abundance or excess of something superfluous.

Gloat(v). – Dwell on one's own success or another's misfortune with smugness or malignant pleasure.

Globetrotter* (adj.). – A person who frequently travels to different places around the world.

Gloss (n). – Shine or luster on a smooth surface.

Glut (n). – An excessively abundant supply of something, (v) – supply or fill to excess.

Glutton* (n). – A person who eats too much; INFORMAL – A person who enjoys having or doing something difficult, unpleasant etc..

Glyptic (adj.). – of or concerning carving or engraving.

Gobble(v). – Eat greedily, hungrily, swallow hurriedly, guzzle, gulp. "Either at home or at a party, one may eat with ease for better digestion of food rather than to gobble".

Goblin* (n). – Mischievous, ugly creature.

Goosebumps* (n). – A state of the skin caused by cold, fear, or excitement, in which small bumps appear on the surface as the hairs become erect; goose pimples.

Gory* (adj.). – Unpleasant or frightening, esp. because they are covered with blood or showing signs of violence.

Gosh (exclamation) – INFORMAL – Used to express surprise or give emphasis; NORTH AMERICAN – used as a euphemism of God.

Gossamer (adj.). – Extremely light and delicate material. "Muslin is quite gossamer fabric to increase ambience of the house in comparison to coarse cotton curtains"

Gouge* (v). – Make a hole in the surface using a sharp object in a rough way.

Gourmet (n). – A connoisseur of good food; a person with a discerning palate of a kind or standard suitable for a gourmet.

Grapple* (v). – Engage in a close fight or struggle without weapons; to get hold of somebody/something and fight with or try to control him/her/it.

Grasp* (v). – Seize and hold firmly; (n). – A firm hold or grip.

Gratuitous (adj.). – (used about an action) lacking any good reason or purpose and often having harmful effects.

Gravitate (v). – Move towards or be attracted to a person or a thing; tend to move towards a centre of gravity or other attractive force.

gregarious. (adj.). – Enjoying the company of other people, outgoing people.

Grimace (n). – An ugly expression on your face that shows that you are angry, disgusting or that something is hurting you.

Grin* (v). – Smile broadly; (n). – A broad smile.

Grip*.(v). – grasp tightly, take and keep firm hold of.

Gripe*(v). – Complaining about something in a persistent, irritating way; (n). – a complaint about somebody/something

Grise (n). – A step (in a flight of stairs); a degree.

Grit (n). – Courage and resolve; strength of character; small loose particles of stone or sand.

Groin (n). – The front part of your body where it joins your legs.

Groove* (n). – A long narrow cut or depression in hard substance.

Grope (v). – Search blindly or uncertainty by feeling with the hands, fondle (someone) for sexual pleasure roughly or clumsily or without the person's consent.

Grotesque (adj). – Comically, repulsively, ugly or distorted; (n). – A very ugly or comically distorted figure or image.

Grovel (v). – Move around on your hands and knees usually when you are looking for something; try too hard to please somebody who is more Important than you or who can give you something that you want.

Grubby (adj.). – Dirty after being used and not washed.

Grudge* (n). – A persistent feeling of ill will or resentment resulting from a past insult or injury.

Grudging (adj.). – Given or allowed reluctantly or resentfully.

Grumpy (adj.). – Bad – tempered, surly or ill – tempered; grouchy.

"A grumpy boss is not a good manager but detrimental for the growth of an organization".

Guile (n). – The ability to be clever but by using dishonest means.

Guile (n). – The ability to be clever but by using dishonest means.

Gulag (n). – Any political labor camp; a camp in the gulag system.

Gulch (n). – A narrow and steep – sided ravine marking the course of a fast stream.

Gulp* (v). – Swallow large amounts of food, drink, etc. quickly; make a swallowing movement because you are afraid, surprised, etc

Gurgle* (v). – Make a sound like water flowing quickly through a narrow space.

Gush* (v). – (used about a liquid) To flow out suddenly and in great quantities; (used about a container/vehicle, etc.) to produce large amounts of liquid

Gusto* (n). – Enjoyment and enthusiasm in doing something; the style in which a work of art is executed.

Gutting (adj.). – Bitterly disappointing or upsetting.

Hackneyed (adj. – (adj.). – (used about phrases, ideas, fashions etc.) Boring because it has been used too often.

Hamstring (n). – Any fine tendons at the back of a person's knee connecting the muscles of one's upper leg to the bones of the lower leg.

Hapless* (adj.). – (especially of a person) Unfortunate.

Harbinger(n). – A person or things that announces or signals the approach of another; a forerunner of something.

Harbor* (n). – a place or the coast where ships can be tied up (moored) and protected from the sea or bad weather.

Harbour (v). – Keep feelings or thoughts secret in your mind for a long time; protect or hide somebody/something that is bad.

Hark* (v). – Listen, hear, obey, give an ear, notice, pay attention.

Harlot (n). – A prostitute; a woman who has many casual sexual encounters or relationships.

Hash out (v). – Talk about (something) : discuss (something).

Hatch* (v). – Thinking of a plan; developing a baby bird.

hearse.(v). – a large car used for carrying a dead person to his/her funeral.

Hearth* (n). – The place where you have an open fire in the house or the area in front of it.

Hector (v). – Talk to (someone) in a bullying way.

Heft* (v). – Lift or carry; (n). – The weight of someone or something.

Hegemon (n). – A supreme leader.

Hegemony(n). – Leadership or dominance, especially by one state or social group over others; leadership.

Hellish* (adj.). – Of or like hell; (adverb). – Terrible, awful.

Helmsman* (n). – A person who steers a ship or boat.

Hem (v). – Turn under and sew the edge of (a piece of cloth), surround and restrict the space or movement of someone or something.

Henpecked* (adj.). – Used to describe a husband who always does what his wife tells him to do.

Herald*(n). – An official employed to oversee state ceremonial, precedence, and the use of armorial bearings.

Heretic (n). – A person whose religious beliefs are believed to be wrong or evil.

Heretical (adj.). – Of or relating to adherence to a religious opinion contrary to church dogma.

Herrenvolk (n). – The German nation was considered by the Nazis to be innately superior to others.

Heterodox (adj.). – Not conforming with accepted or orthodox standards or beliefs.

Hewer*(n). – A person who cuts wood, stone, or other materials.

Hiatus (n). – A pause or break in continuity in a sequence or activity; prosody. Grammar – a break in two vowels coming together but not in the same syllable, as in the ear and cooperate.

Hiatus. (n). – A pause or break in continuity in a sequence or activity when nothing happens.

Hiccup(n). – A temporary or minor problem or setback.

Hierarchical*(adj.). – Of the nature of a hierarchy; arranged in order of rank.

Highbrow* (adj.). – Interested in or concerned with matters that many people would find too serious to be interesting.

Hind* (adj.). – (used about an animal's legs, etc.) At the back.

Hindsight (n). – Understanding of a situation or event only after it has happened or developed.

Hinterland (n). – The remote areas of a country away from the coast or the banks of major rivers; an area lying beyond what is visible or known.

Hoary (adj.). – Grayish white, (of a person). – Old and having gray or white hair, used in the names of animals and plants covered with whitish fur or short hair.

Hobble* (v). – Walk in an awkward way, typically because of pain from an injury.

Hobson's choice (n). – A choice of taking what is available or nothing at all.

Hoe* (n). – A garden tool with a long handle that is used for turning the soil and for removing unwanted plants.

Hog* (n). – A male pig that is kept for its meat; (v). – Take or keep too much or aloof something for yourself.

Holler (v). – INFORMAL – Give a loud shout or cry; (n). – A loud cry or shout.

Holocaust. (n). – A destruction or a slaughter on a mass scale, especially caused by fire or nuclear war; HISTORICAL – A Jewish sacrificial offering that was burned completely on an altar.

Holster* (n). – A small case usually made of leather and fixed on a belt or a strap, used for carrying a gun.

Homogenize* (v). – Make uniform or similar; subject (milk) to a process in which fat droplets are emulsified and the cream does not separate.

Hone* (v). – Smooth and sharpen (a blade), refine or perfect (something) over a period of time; (n). – A whetstone, especially one used to sharpen razors.

Honeycomb* (n). – A structure of holes (cells) with six sides, in which bees keep their eggs and the honey they produce.

Honorific (n). – A title or word implying or expressing respect; (adj.). – Given as a mark of respect but having few or no duties.

Hoofprint (n). – A mark or hollow made by a hoof.

Hornet's nest (n). – A troublesome or hazardous situation.

Horrendous (adj.). – So bad as to be shocking; extremely unpleasant.

Hotchpotch* (n). – A confused mixture, a mutton stew with mixed vegetables.

Hubbub. (n). – A busy, noisy situation; a chaotic din caused by a crowd of people.

Hubris (n). – Excessive pride or self confidence.

Huddle* (v). – Crowd together, nestle closely; heap together in a disorderly manner; (n). – a close group of people or things.

Humbug (n). – Deceptive or false talk of behavior; British – a boiled sweet, especially one flavored with peppermint.

Hump* (n). – A large round lump, for example on the back of an animal who lives in the desert (camel).

Hunchback (n). – A person with a back that has a round lump on it.

Hunker (v). – Squat or crouch down low; apply oneself seriously to a task.

Hurtle (v). – Move or cause to move at a high speed, typically in an uncontrolled manner.

Hustle* (v). – Push roughly, jostle, obtain illicitly or by forceful action.

Hymn* (n). – A religious song that Christians sing together in church, etc.; Sanskrit verses while performing Havan around fire by Hindus.

Hyphenate* (v). – join two words together with a hyphen.

Hypochondriac(n). – A person who is abnormally anxious about their health; (adj.). – Another term for hypochondriacal.

Iconoclasm (v). – The rejection or destruction of religious images as heretical; the doctrine of iconoclasts.

Iconoclast (n). – A person who criticizes accepted idea

Iconography. (n). – A collection of illustrations and portraits, the visual images and symbols used in a work of art, or their study.

Ideation (n). – Refers to the process of developing and conveying prescriptive ideas to others.

Idiosyncrasy (n). – A person's particular way of behaving, thinking, etc., especially when it is unusual; an unusual characteristic.

Idolatry (n). – The worship of idols; extreme admiration, love, or reverence for something or someone.

Ignoble.(adj.). – Being below the normal standards of human decency and dignity.

Ignominy* (n). – Public shame and embarrassment; a loss of honor.

Ignoramus* (n). – A person who does not know much.

Illiberalism (n). – Opposition to or lack of liberalism.

Imbecility (adj.). – The quality or state of being very stupid or foolish.

Imbibe* (v). – FORMAL – Absorb something, especially information, to drink something, especially alcoholic drinks.

Imbroglio (n). – An extremely confused, complicated or embarrassing situation.

Imbue (v). – Inspire or permeate with (a feeling or quality).

Imbue* (v). – inspire or permeate with (a feeling or quality.

Immunization* (n). – The action of making a person or animal immune to infection, typically by inoculation.

Impale (v). – To push sharp pointed objects through somebody or something.

Impeccable (adverb). – In accordance with the highest standards; faultlessly.

Impediment* (n). – Hindrance/obstruction in doing something.

Impenetrable (adj.). – Impossible to understand, impossible to enter or go through

Impertinent* (adj.) – Rude, not showing proper respect

Impetuosity (n). – Marked by impulsive vehemence or passion, impulsive, hot headed.

Impetus* (n). – Something that encourages something else to happen.

Implicit* (adj.). – Complete, total; not expressed in a direct way but understood by the people involved.

Implore*(v). – Beg someone earnestly or desperately to do something.

Impregnable (adj.). – (of a fortified position) Unable to be captured or broken into.

Impregnate* (v). – Soak or saturate (something) with a substance; make (a woman or female animal) pregnant.

Impromptu* (adj.). – (done) Without being prepared or organized.

Impudence (n). – Impertinence, ebullience, shameful acts.

Impulse*(adj.). – Acting or done without forethought.

In a trice. – Phrase in English – In a moment; very quickly. “Your discussion on gender equality is very interesting, but don’t conclude in a trice”.

Inalienable (adj.). – Not subject to being taken away from or give away by the possessor

Inanimate* (adj.) – Not alive in the way that people, animals and plants are, cold, dead, defunct, dull, extinct, inert, lifeless.

Incandescent* (adj.). – Giving out light as a result of being heated to a high temperature.

Incarceration (n). – The state of being confined to prison.

Incessant* (adj.). – Never stopping (and usually moving).

Incestuous* (adj.). – Involving illegal sex between members of the same family.

Incinerator* (v). – An apparatus for burning waste material.

Incipient (adj.). – Just beginning, nascent, developing.

Incongruity* (n). – Dissimilarity, discordance, contrariety in the sense of disparity, incompatibility, the state of being incongruous.

Incorrigible* (adj.). – (used about a person or his/her behavior) Very bad; too bad to be corrected or improved.

Incredulous (adj.). – (of a person or their manner) Unwilling or unable to believe something.

Incriminate (v). – Provide evidence that sb (somebody) is guilty of a crime.

indefatigable.(adj.). – Never giving up or getting tired of doing something.

Indelible* (adj.). – FIGURATIVE – That cannot be removed or washed out.

Indictment* (n). – A thing that serves to illustrate that a system or situation is bad and deserves to be condemned; NORTH AMERICAN – A formal charge or accusation of a serious crime.

Indignant* (adj.) – Feeling or showing anger or annoyance at what is perceived as unfair treatment.

Indignation (n). – Anger or annoyance provoked by what is perceived as unfair treatment.

Indomitable (adj.). – Impossible to subdue or defeat.

Inebriated* (adj.). – Affected by alcohol; drunk. "Driving while inebriated is a crime. We may avoid driving under the influence of alcohol".

Inebriety (n). – Drunkenness, especially habitual intoxication.

Ineluctable (adj.). – Unable to be resisted or avoided; inescapable, unavoidable, unpreventable, unstoppable, sure, certain.

Inept* (adj.). – Clumsy; having or showing no skill.

Inexorable (adj.). – Impossible to stop or prevent, unrelenting.

Inexplicable* (adj.). – That cannot be explained

Inexplicably* (adverb). – In a way that cannot be explained or accounted for.

Infantilize(v). – Treat (someone) as a child or in a way which denies their maturity in age or experience.

Infatuated (adj.). – having a very strong feeling of love or attraction for somebody/something that does not last long and makes you unable to think about anything else.

Infidelity* (n). – The act of not being faithful to your wife or husband by having a sexual relationship with somebody else.

Infinitesimal* (adj.). – An indefinitely small quantity; a value approaching zero.

Inflection (n). – The modulation of intonation or pitch in the voice, a change in the form of the word(typically the ending) to express grammatical function or attitude such as tense, mood, person, number, ease and gender.

Infodemic (n). – Rapid and far reaching spread of both accurate and inaccurate information about something, such as a disease; as facts, rumors, and fears mix and disperse.

Infraction (n). – A violation or infringement of a law or agreement.

Infringe* (v). – Actively break the terms of (a law, agreement etc.; act or so to limit or undermine.

Ingenuity (n). – Inventiveness, correctness, cleverness, imagination, resourcefulness.

Ingest (v). – Eat or drink something.

Ingrain (v). – Firmly fix or establish (a habit, belief, or attitude in a person.

Ingratiate (v). – Make yourself liked by doing or saying things that will please people, especially people who might be useful to you.

Ingress(n). – The action or fact of going or entering; the capacity or right of entrance, the arrival of the sun, moon or a planet in a specified constellation or part of the sky.

Inhabit (n). – Occupy (of a person, animal, or group), live in or occupy a place or environment.

Inimical* (adj.). – Tending to obstruct or harm; unfriendly; hostile.

Iniquitous (adj.). – Grossly unfair and morally wrong.

Injunction* (n). – Law – A judicial order restraining a person from beginning or continuing an action threatening or invading the legal right of another, or compelling a person to do a certain act.

Innards (v). – The internal working of a device or a machine.

Innate* (adj.). – New born; natural.

Innocuous (adj.) – Not harmful or offensive.

Innuendo.(n). – An allusive or oblique remark or hint, typically a suggestive or disparaging one;

Inscrutable (adj.). – Impossible to understand or interpret.

Insidious (adj.). – Processing in a gradual, subtle way, but with very harmful effects.

Insinuation (n). – An unpleasant hint or suggestion of something bad.

Insipid (adj.). – Having too little taste, flavor or color, tasteless.

Insolence* (n). – Rude and disrespectful behavior.

Insouciance (n). – Casual lack of concern, indifference.

Insuperable* (adj.). – FORMAL – (used about a problem etc.) Impossible to solve.

Insurmountable* (adj.). – Great to be overcome.

Intaglio (n). – A design incised or engraved into a material.

Intangible* (adj.). – Unable to be touched or grasped; not having physical presence.

Intercede* (v). – Intervene on behalf of another.

Internecine (adj.). – Destructive to both sides in a conflict.

Interregnum (n). An arrival or pause between two periods of office or other things; the period in English history from the execution of Charles I in 1649 to the restoration of Charles II in 1660.

Intertwine* (v). – Twist or twine together, connect or link (two or more things) together.

Intractable (adj.). – (used about a person or a problem) Extremely difficult to control or deal with.

Intransigence (n). – Refusal to change one's views or to agree about something.

Intransigent (adj.). – Unwilling or refusing to change one's views or to agree about something; (n). – An intransigent person.

Intricacy* (n). – The complicated parts or details of something, the quality of having complicated parts, details or patterns.

Intrigue* (v). – Arouse curiosity or interest or fascinate; make secret plans to do something illicit or detrimental to someone.

Inundate (v). – Overwhelm (someone) with things or people to be dealt with.

Investiture (n). – The action of formally investigating a person with honor or rank.

"It is always better to be gentle, sober with good managerial skill rather than feeling invincible"

Invincible* (adj.). – Too powerful to be defeated or overcome.

Inviolable(adj.). – Never to be broken, infringed, or dishonored.

invocation*.(n). – The act of making somebody feel a particular emotion or remember something, the act of asking for help, especially from a god law or person in authority; the act of referring to something.

Involution* (n). – The shrinkage of an organ in old age when inactive, e.g. of the uterus after childbirth.

Inweigh (v). – A peak or weigh about (something) with great hostility.

Irrepressible (adj.). – Not able to be controlled or restrained, inextinguishable, unquenchable.

Irreverence (n). – Disrespect, disregard, rudeness toward someone, coarseness, contempt.

Irreverent (adj.) – Showing a lack of respect for people or things that are generally taken seriously.

Iscern* (v). – Recognise or find out.

Jaded (adj.). – Bored or lacking enthusiasm.

Jangle* (v). – Make or cause to make a ringing metallic sound, typically a discount one.

Janitor* (n). – A caretaker, a person employed to look after a building.

Jargon* (n). – Special or technical words that are used by a particular group of people in a particular profession and that other people do not understand.

Jarring*(adj.). – Clashing in a striking or a shocking way.

Jaunty (adj.). – Having or expressing a lively, cheerful, and self confident manner.

Jaw – clenching* (v). – When you clench your teeth or they clench, usually because you are angry or upset.

Jeering* (adj.) – Making rude and mocking remarks, typically in a loud voice.

Jetsam (n). – Unwanted material or goods that have been thrown overboard from a ship and washed ashore, especially material that has been discarded to lighten the vessel.

Jibe* (n). – An insulting or a mocking remark; a taunt.

Jingoism (n). – DEROGATORY – Extreme patriotism, especially in the form of aggressive or warlike foreign policy.

Jinx (v). – Bring curse; (n). – Bad luck or things that people believe bring bad luck to someone/something.

Jostle* (v). – Push, elbow, or bump against (someone) roughly, typically in a crowd; (v). – The action of pushing .

Joust*(v). – Compete closely for superiority; (of a medieval knight) engage in a sporting contest in which two opponents on horseback fight with lances.

Jousting (n). A medieval sporting contest in which two contestants on horseback, typically Knights, fight with lancers.

Juggernaut (n). – A huge, powerful one and overwhelming force; a large heavy vehicle, especially an articulated lorry.

Jumble (v). – Mix things together in a confused and untidy way, an untidy group of things.

Juror (n). – A member of a jury; HISTORICAL – A person taking an oath, especially one of allegiance.

Jutting (adj.). – Projecting, protruding, the jutting limb of a tree

Juxtapose (v). – Place or deal with close together for contrasting effect.

Kaftan* (n). – A man's long belted tunic, worn in countries of the Near East; a loose shirt or top; a woman's long loose dress

Ken* (n). – One's range of knowledge or understanding, (v). – Know.

Kerfuffle (n). – A commotion or fuss, especially caused by conflicting views.

Kimono* (n). – A long, loose traditional Japanese robe with wide sleeves, tied with a sash; a garment similar to a kimono worn elsewhere as a dressing gown.

Kleptocratic (adj.). – Government by those who seek chiefly status and personal gains at the cost of government.

Knack (n). – A special skill or ability that you have naturally or can learn.

Knack* (n). – An acquired or natural skill at doing something; a tendency to do something.

Kryptonite(n). – Something that can seriously weaken or harm a particular person or thing.

Labyrinth (n). – A complicated irregular network of passages or paths in which it is difficult to find one's way; a maze; ANATOMY – A complex

Lacerate (v). – Tear or make deep cuts in (flesh or skin), criticize forcefully or severely.

"If you come across people lacerating each other, you should call the police and wait on the spot"

Lackadaisical (adj.). – Lacking enthusiasm and determination; carelessly lazy.

Lackluster* (adj.). – Lacking in vitality, force or conviction, uninspired or uninspiring, dull.

Laconic (adj.). – (of a person, speech or style of writing) Using very few words.

Laggard* (n). – A person who makes slow progress and falls behind.

Laissez – faire (n). – The policy of having things take their own course, without interfering; abstention by governments from interfering in the working of the market; liberal.

Laity (n). – Lay people, as distinct from the clergy; ordinary people, as distinct from professionals or experts.

Lampoon (v). – Publicly criticize (someone or something) by using ridicule, irony or sarcasm.

Lance*(n). – A long weapon with a wooden shaft and a pointed steel head, formerly used by a horseman in charging.

Lancer (n). – A soldier of a cavalry regiment armed with lance; a quadrille for eight or sixteen pairs.

Lancet (n). – A small, broad two edged surgical knife or blade with a sharp point.

Languid.(adj.). – Weak or faint from illness or fatigue; (of a person, manner, or gesture) having or showing a disinclination for physical exertion or effort.

Languidly (adj.). – Lacking energy or disinclined to exert effort; lifeless, feeling languid from a fever; slow – moving or weak in force.

Lanky* (adj.). – (of a person) Ungracefully thin and tall.

Largesse* (n). – Generosity in bestowing money or gifts upon others; money or gifts given generously. "Different political parties promise to give various kinds of largesse during election times". What do you think ?

Lascivious. (adj.) – Feeling or revealing an overt sexual interest or desire.

Lasya (adj.). – Beauty, happiness, enchanting, and grace; a delicate and feminine dance form.

Lean (v). – Cause something to rest against; incline from the perpendicular and rest for support against (something); be in or move into a sloping position. Lethal* (adj.). – Very harmful or destructive; sufficient to cause death.

Leapfrog* (v). Passover, surpass or overtake another to move into a leading or dominant position.

Leaven (n). – A substance, typically yeast, that is used in dough to make it rise, a pervasive influence that modifies something or transforms it for the better.

Lecherous (adj.) – Having or showing excessive or offensive sexual look.

Ledge hammer* (n). – A large heavy hammer used for such jobs as breaking rocks and driving in fence posts.

Leeway (n). – The amount of freedom to move or act that is available.

Leitmotif (n). – A recurrent theme throughout a musical or literary composition, associated with a particular person, idea or situation.

Levee (n). – An embankment built to allow the overflow of water.

Lexicon*. (n). – The study of the vocabulary of a language.

Licentious (adj.). – FORMAL – Showing a complete lack of moral discipline and standard, especially in relation to sex.

Limbo* (n). – A situation in which you are not sure what to do next, cannot take action etc., especially because you are waiting for somebody to make a decision.

Limp* (v). – Walk with difficulty, typically because of a damaged or stiff leg or foot; (n). – A tendency to limp; a gait Impeded by injury or stiffness.

Limpid* (adj.). – Something (often liquid) that is clear, serene and bright.

Linchpin* (n). – A person or thing vital to an enterprise or organization; a pin passed through the end of an axle to keep a wheel in position.

Linger* (v). – Stay somewhere or do something for longer than usual.

Liquidate (v). – Close a business because no money is left, destroy or remove somebody/something that causes problems.

Lisp (n). – A speech fault in which 's' is pronounced as 'th'.

Liturgical (adj.). – Related to public worship or liturgy.

Liveried (adj.). – Wearing a special uniform

Livid.(adj.). – Furiously angry, dark bluish gray in color.

Loath* (adj.). – Not willing to do something.

Lobotomy (n). – A form of psychosurgery, a neurosurgical treatment of a mental disorder that involves severing connections in the brain's prefrontal cortex.

Logjam* (n). – A crowded mass of logs blocking a river, a situation that seems irreversible.

Loll (v). – Sit, lie, or stand in a lazy, relaxed way; stick out (one's tongue) so that it hangs loosely; of a part of the body) hang loosely; droop.

Loom* (v). – Appear as a vague form, especially one that is large or threatening; (of an event regarded as threatening) seem about to happen.

Ludicrous (adj.). – So foolish, unreasonable, or out of place as to be amusing.

Lumber* (v). – Move in a slow, heavy, awkward way

Lurk* (v). – Be or remain hidden so as to wait in ambush for someone or something; (n). – a profitable scheme, a dodge or stratagem.

Lurking* (adj.). – Remaining hidden so as to wait in ambush; (of an unpleasant quality) present in a latent or discernible state, although still presenting a threat.

Luscious(adj.). – (of food or drink) Having a pleasantly rich, sweet taste, appealing, strongly to the senses.

Lute (n). – A plucked stringed instrument with a long neck bearing frets and a rounded body with a flat front, rather like a halved egg in shape.

Lyre (n). – Modern u shaped instruments with strings fixed on a crossbar found mainly in East Africa.

Macabre (adj.). – Unpleasant and frightening because it is connected with death.

Machiavellian (adj.). – Cunning, scheming and unscrupulous.

Machismo (n). – Strong or aggressive masculine pride.

Madonna* (n). – Lady – used as a form of respectful address, obsolete, an Italian lady, virgin Mary, morally pure and chaste woman.

Maelstrom(n). – A powerful whirlpool in the sea or river.

Maim (v). – Hurt so badly that part of his/her body can no longer be used. .

Malaise* (n). – A general feeling of discomfort, illness or unease.

Maleficent (adj.). – Causing harm or destruction, especially by supernatural means.

Malevolent (adj.). – Having or showing a desire to harm others.

Malicious* (adj.). – Characterized by malice, intending to do harm.

Manacle (n). – One of two metal bands joined by a chain for fastening a person's hands or ankles.

Mandamus (n). – A judicial writ issued as a command to an interior court or ordering a person to perform a public or statutory duty.

Mandarin (n). – By far the largest of the seven or ten Chinese dialect groups spoken by over 730 M people; bureaucrats or an official who tends to make things complicated and who wields a lot of power.

Mane* (n). – The long hair on the neck of a horse or male lion.

Maneuver (n). – A movement or series of moves requiring skill and care.

mangle(v). – Destroy or severely damage by tearing or crushing, ruin or spoil (a text, piece of music, etc..

Mangle*(v). – Destroy or severely damage by treating or crushing.

Manifest* (v). – Show something or to be shown clearly, obviously.

Manor (n). – BRITISH – A large country house with lands; INFORMAL – the district covered by a police station.

Marauder. (n). – One who roams from place to place for raids in search of plunder.

Marinate*.(v). – (of food) Undergo marination; soak (meat, fish, or other food) to make it softer.

Marquee* (n). – A large tent used for social or commercial function; a canopy projecting over the entrance to a theater, hotel or other building.

Martian* (adj.). – Imaginary creature from Mars

Masochism (n). – The enjoyment of pain, or of what most people would find unpleasant.

Masquerade (n). – A way of behaving that hides the truth or somebody's true feelings.

Mast* (n) – A tall wooden or metal pole for a flag, a ship's sails etc.; a tall pole that is used for sending out radio or television signals.

Matriarch (n). – A woman who is the head of a family or tribe; an older woman who is powerful within a family or organization. "In many parts of India, the oldest lady is considered the Matriarch of the family".

Matted.* (adj.). – (used especially about hair) Forming a thick mass, especially because it is wet and/or dirty.

Mayonnaise* (n). – Thick creamy dressing consisting of egg yolks beaten with oil and vinegar and seasoned.

Maze (n). – A system of paths which is designed to confuse you so that it is difficult to find your way out.

Meander (v). – (used about a river, road. etc.) Have a lot of curves and bends, (used about a person or animal) to walk or travel slowly or without any definite direction.

Meddle* (v). – Take too much interest in someone's private affairs or to touch something that does not belong to you.

Medley* (n). – A varied mixture of people or things; (adj.). – mixed; motley; (v). – Archaic – Make a medley of; intermix.

Megalomania (n). – A mental disorder or condition in which a person has an exaggerated belief in their own power or importance.

Megalomaniac (n). – A person who has an obsessive desire for power; (adj.). – Exhibiting megalomania.

Melancholy (n). – A feeling of pensive sadness, typically with no obvious cause; (adj.). – Feeling of sadness and a pensive mood.

Meliorate* (v). – make (something bad or unsatisfactory) better.

Mellifluous. (adj.). – (used about music, somebody's voice etc.) Sounding sweet and smooth; pleasant.

Mellow* (v). – Soften; (adj.). – (used about colors and sounds) Soft and pleasant; (used about people) Calm and relaxed.

Memorabilia (n). – Objects kept or collected because of their association with memorable people or events; ARCHAIC – memorable or noteworthy observations or writings.

Mendicant* (n). – A beggar; given to begging.

Mercurial* (adj.). – Subject to sudden and unpredictable changes of mood or mind; (n). – a drug or other compound containing mercury.

Meritocracy* (n). – A society governed by people selected according to merit; a ruling or influential class of educated or able people.

Messiness*(adj.). – A state of confusion and disorderliness.

Meta – analysis* (n). – Examination of data from a number of independent studies of the same subject, in order to determine overall trends.

Metaphor (n). – A word or phrase that is used in an imaginative way to show that somebody/something has the same qualities as another thing.

Metaphysical* (adj.). – Related to metaphysics, of or characteristic of the metaphysical poets.

Metaphysics* (n). – The branch of philosophy that studies the fundamental nature of reality; the first principles of being, identity and change, space and time, cause and effect, necessity and possibility and also deals with logic, and ethics.

Microvita(n). – Subtle sub – atomic living entities that travel throughout the universe, creating bodies and minds.

Middling* (adverb). – Moderately or fairly; (n). – Bulk foods of medium grade, especially flour of medium fineness; (adj.). – Moderate or average in size, amount or rank.

Miff (n). – Force to act or speak prematurely or unwillingly; a fit of ill humor.

Miffed* (adj.). – A little angry or upset.

Milch cow (n). – A person or organization that is a source of easy profit.

Milieu* (n). – The social environment that you live or work in; environment.

Miniscule (adj.). – Extremely small; tiny; of or in lower – case letters, as distinct from capitals; (n). – Miniscule script.

Minnow (n). – A small or insignificant person/ organization.

Miranda (adj.). – Denoting or relating to the duty of the police to inform a person taken into custody of their right to legal counsel and the right to remain silent under questioning.

Mire (v). – cause to become stuck in mud, cover or spatter with mud, involve someone or something in (a difficult situation.

Misogynist (n). – A man who hates women.

Mitigate* (v). – Make something bad less severe or painful.

Mitigation* (n). – The action of reducing the severity, seriousness, or painfulness of something.

Mockery* (n). – An absurd misrepresentation or limitation of something; teasing and contemptuous language directed at a particular person.

Modicum* (n). – A small quantity of a particular thing, especially something desirable or valuable.

Modus Vivendi (n). – An arrangement or agreement made between people, institutions or countries with different opinions to exist and work together without disagreeing.

Mollycoddle (v). – Treat (someone) in an indulgent or overprotective way.

Momentous* (adj.). – Of great importance or significance, especially in having a bearing on future events.

Monism (n). – The doctrine that only one supreme being exists; a theory or doctrine that denies the existence of a distinction or duality in a particular sphere, such as that between matter and mind, or God and the world.

Monopolistic (adj.). – Relating to a person or business that has exclusive possession or control of the supply of or trade in a commodity or service.

Monotheism (n). – The belief that there is only one God.

Monotheistic (adj.). – Relating to or characterized by the belief that there is only one God.

Mooing (n). – Make the long, deep sound that a cow makes.

Mooring* (n). – A place wherever a boat or ship is moored; the ropes, chains, or anchors by or to which a boat, ship is moored.

Morass* (n). – An area of low soft wet marshy land; a complicated and dangerous situation that is especially difficult to escape from. "While walking in deep forests, one may be careful in areas near wet marshy lands, which convert into morasses".

morbidity* (n). – The condition of suffering from a disease or suffering.

Morose* (n). – An alphabet or code in which letters are represented by combinations of long and short light or sound signals.

Morph* (v). – To develop a new appearance or change into something different; to make somebody/something do this; to make an image change smoothly into another image using computer animation; to change in this way; (n). – The way that a morphine is represented in phonetics.

Morsel* (n). – A very small piece of something, usually food.

Mortality* (n). – The number of deaths in one period of time or in one place, the fact that nobody can live forever.

Mortification (n). – Strong feelings of embarrassment, humiliation. "These days teachers cannot even stare at students as they get the feeling of mortification".

Mortify (v). – Make somebody feel very embarrassed; engrossed.

moss* (n). – A very small, green or yellow plant that grows especially in wet earth, or on rocks, walls, and tree trunks.

Motile (adj.). – Capable of moving spontaneously and independently.

Mottled (adj.). – Marked with shapes of different colors without a regular pattern.

Muck* (n). – The waste from farm animals, used to make plants grow better, INFORMAL – dirt or mud.

Muddled* (adj.). – Not arranged in order, untidy, confused, not clear or coherent.

Mull* (adj. – Think about (a proposal, fact, or request) and think deeply and at length.

Mundane (adj.). – Ordinary; not interesting or exciting.

Munificence (n). – Giving or bestowing with extraordinary liberty, very liberal in giving.

Munificent (Adj.). – Characterized by or displaying great generosity.

Muppet (n). – An incompetent or foolish person.

Murky* (adj.). – Dark and gloomy, especially due to thick mist; obscure or morally questionable.

Mutate* (v). – Change in form or nature.

Mutter*(v). – Say something in a low or barely audible voice, especially in dissatisfaction or irritation.

Muzzle* (n). – The projecting part of the face, including the nose and mouth, of an animal such as a dog or horse; the opened part of the barrel of a firearm; (v). – Put a muzzle on (an animal).

Myriad (n). – FORMAL – A very large number of things.

Mystical* (adj.). – Connected with the spirit; strange and powerful.

Mysticism (n). – The belief that you can reach complete truth and knowledge of God or gods by prayer, thought and development of the spirit.

Nagging (adj.). – (of a person) Constantly harassing someone to do something; persistently painful or worrying.

Naivete (n). – Lack of experience, wisdom or judgment, innocence.

Narcissist (n). – A person who has an excessive interest in or admiration of themselves.

Narcissistic (adj.). – Having or showing excessive interest in or admiration of oneself and one's physical appearance, vain.

Narwhal (n). – A small Arctic whale, the male of which has a long forward-pointing spirally twisted tusk developed from one of its teeth.

Nativism (n). – The policy of protecting the interests of native – born or established inhabitants against those of immigrants; philosophy – the theory of concepts, mental capacities, and mental structures.

Naught (pronoun). – ARCHAIC – Nothing; (n). – NORTH AMERICAN – the digit 0 ; nought.

Nemesis (n). – FORMAL – A punishment or defeat that somebody deserves and cannot avoid.

Nerdy* (adj.). – Characterized by an obsessive interest in something, especially technology; Informal – unfashionable and socially inept or boringly studious.

Nescience (n). – Lack of knowledge or awareness, ignorance.

Nestle (v). – Go in a position where you are comfortable, protected or hidden, strangled, snuggled.

Netherlands* (n). Low lying country, the old name Holland from Houtland or Wooded Land.

Neuroticism (n). – A personality trait characterized by instability, anxiety, and aggression.

Nibble (v). – Take small bites out of; show cautious interest in a commercial activity.

Niche* (n). – A comfortable or suitable position in life or employment; a specialized segment of the market for a particular kind of products, or service; (adj.). – Denoting products, services, or interests that appeal to a small, specialized section of the population.

Niggardly (adj.). – Petty in giving or spending, miserly, stingy.

Nightmare* (n). – A frightening or unpleasant dream, an experience that is very unpleasant or frightening.

Nightmarish* (n). – Very frightening or unpleasant; of the nature of a nightmare.

Nihilism (n). – The belief that nothing in the world has real existence; the rejection of all religious and moral principles in the life that life is meaningless.

Nihilistic (adj.). – Rejecting moral principles of all religions in the belief that life is meaningless.

Nimble*.(adj.). – Quick and light in movement or action; agile; (of the mind) able to think and understand quickly.

Nip (v). – Give somebody/something a quick bite or to quickly squeeze a piece of somebody skin between your thumb or finger.

Nix* (v). – Cancel something, stop something from happening.

Noblesse (adj.). – French Phrase – privilege, noble birth or condition.

Nocturnal* (adj.). – Awake and active at night and asleep during the day.

Non partisan (adj.). – Not supported or controlled by a political party, special interest group, or the like.

Nonchalantly (adverb). – In a casual way that shows a relaxed lack of concern or interest.

Nook* (n). – A small quiet place or corner (in a house, garden, etc.).

Noose (n). – A circle that is tied in the end of a rope and that gets smaller as one end of the rope is pulled.

Normality* (n) – State of being normal, conformity to the standard, typical, or average level, rate, condition, or set of conditions, characteristics, behaviour etc; CHEMISTRY – desired concentration of a solution but replaced by molarity at present

Nostalgia* (n). – A sentimental longing or wistful affection for a period in the past.

Nuance* (n). – A subtle difference in or shade of meaning, expression or sound.

Nudge* (v). – Touch or push somebody/something with your elbow.

Nugget* (n). – A small lump of a valuable metal or mineral, especially gold, found in its natural state in the earth; any useful idea or fact. "In the early nineteenth century, people from Europe other countries started rushing towards California for gold nuggets".

Numbing* (adj.). – Depriving one of feeling or responsiveness.

Nymph (n). – (in Greek and Roman stories) A spirit in the form of a young woman that lives in rivers, woods, etc.

Oar* (n). – A long pole with a wide flat part at one end, used for rowing a boat.

Obduracy* (adj.). – The state of being obstinate or hardhearted; stubborn.

Obdurate (v). – Subbornly refusing to change one's opinion or course of action; starlit.

Obfuscate (v). – Make something unclear and more difficult to understand.

Obfuscation (n). The action of making something obscure, unclear,or unintelligible.

Oblation* (n). – A thing presented or offered to God; Christian Church – The presentation of bread and wine to God in the Eucharist.

Obliterate* (v). – Destroy utterly; wipe out; make invisible or indistinct, conceal or cover; cancel (something, especially a postage stamp) to prevent further use.

Oblivious* (adj.). – Not aware of, or concerned about what is happening around one.

Oblong* (adj., n). – Rectangle – a shape with two long and two short sides.

Obscenity* (n). – Sexual words or acts that shock people and cause offense; sexual language or behavior, especially in books, etc., which shocks people and causes offense.

Obscure* (adj.). – Not well known; not easy to see or understand.

Obsequious (adj.). – Obedient or attentive to an excessive or servile degree.

Obsequiously (adverb). – Characterized by or showing servile obedience and excessive eagerness to please.

Obsidian (n). – A hard, dark, glasslike volcanic rock formed by the rapid solidification of lava without crystallization.

Occidental* (adj.). – Western, lying towards, near, or facing the west.

Occipital (adj.). – Relating to or in the back of the head.

Occult science (adj.). – Knowledge of the hidden, knowledge of the paranormal.

Octogenarian*(n). – A person who is between 80 and 89 years old.

Odyssey (n). – A long and eventful or adventurous journey or experience.

Ogle (v). – Stare at in a lecherous manner; a lecherous look.

Olfactory (adj.). – Connected with the sense of smell.

Oligarch (n). – A very rich business leader with a great deal of political influence.

Ominous* (Adj.). – Suggesting that something bad is going to happen, threatening

Omniscient (adj.). – Knowing everything.

One-upmanship (n). – The technique or practice of giving an advantage or feeling of superiority over another person.

Onerous. (adj.). – Involving heavy obligations; (of a task or responsibility) involving a great deal of effort), trouble or difficulty.

Opprobrium (n). – A harsh criticism or censure.

Opulence (n). – Abundance, richness, robustness.

Orchestrate* (v). – Plan or coordinate the elements of (a situation) to produce a desired effect; arrange or score (music) for orchestral performance.

Ordain* (v). – Make (someone) a priest or minister.

Orgy (n). – A wild party characterized by excessive drinking and indiscriminate sexual activity.

Ornery (adj.). – Bad – tempered or difficult to deal with.

Ostentation (n). – The pretentious or showy display of wealth and luxury, designed to impress.

Ostentatious (adj.). – Expensive or noticeable in a way that is intended to impress other people.

Ostentatiously (adverb). – Showy way designed to impress.

Otorhinolaryngologist (adj.). – A medical speciality concerned especially with ear, nose and throat.

Outlandish (adj.). – Looking or sounding bizarre or unfamiliar; ARCHAIC – foreign or alien.

Outmaneuver* (v). – Evade (an opponent) by moving faster with greater agility.

Outrageous* (adj.). – Shockingly bad or excessive; very bold and unusual and rather shocking.

Overarching (adj.). – Comprehensive or all – embarrassing.

Overawe (v). – Impress (someone) so much that they are silent or inhibited, intimidate, daunt, cow, potentiate.

Overt (adj.). – FORMAL – Done in an open way and not secretly.

Paean (n). – A song of praise or trump; a creative work expressing enthusiastic praise.

Pagan (adj.). – Having religious beliefs that do not belong to any of the main world religions.

Palanquin (n). – A big covered box – like vehicle usually with a seat for one person. It is attached to poles and is carried on shoulders by four or six men,

Palimpsest (n). – A manuscript or piece of writing material on which later writing has been superimposed on effaced earlier writing; something reused or altered but still bearing visible traces of its earlier writing.

Pall* (v). – Become less interesting or important, glut, gorge, sate, satiate, surfeit.

Palpable (adj.). – That is easily felt by the senses or the mind; that can be handled or touched.

Pan* (n). – A metal container with a handle or handles that is used for cooking food in; the contents of a pan.

Pander (v). – gratify or indulge (an immoral or distasteful desire or taste of a person with such a desire or taste.

Pandy (v). – Gratify or indulge (an immoral and distasteful desire or taste of a person with such a desire or taste.

Panegyric (n). – Formal – A piece of writing or speech praising somebody/something.

Pang. (n). – A strong feeling of emotional or physical pain.

Pantheism (n). – The belief that God exists in all natural things, belief in all gods or worshiping a large number of gods.

Pantheistic* (adj.). – A doctrine that equates God with the forces and laws of the universe, the worship of all gods of different creeds.

Pantheon (n). – A group of particularly respected, famous, or important people.

Pany (adj.). – Marketable; (n). – ware, merchandise; a commodity.

Papyrus (n). – A material prepared in ancient Egypt from the pithy stem of a water plant, used in sheets throughout the ancient Mediterranean world for writing or painting on and also for making articles such as rope; the tall aquatic sedge from which papyrus is obtained, native to central Africa and the Nile valley.

Paradox (n). – A person or a thing that combines contradictory features or qualities; a seemingly absurd or contradictory statement or proposition which when investigated may prove to be well founded or true.

Paragon* (n). – A perfect person; An ideal example of a particular good quality.

Paranoia (n). – Unjustified suspicion and mistrust of other people.

Paranoid (adj.). – Overly suspicious, unreasonably distrustful, confused.

Paranoja (n). – A type of mental illness in which you wrongly believe that other people want to harm you; a feeling of fear and suspicion of other people.

Paranormal (adj.). – (used about events or subjects) Which cannot be explained by science or reason and that seems to be strange or mysterious.

Paraphernalia* (n). – A large number of different objects that you need for a particular purpose.

Parch* (v). – Make or become dry through intense heat.

Parched* (adj.). – Dried out with heat; Informal – extremely thirsty.

Pariah (n). – An outcast, HISTORICAL – a member of an indigenous people of southern India originally functioning as ceremonial drummers but later having a low cast.

Parlance* (n). – Formal way of expressing your style of using words of a group of people.

Parochial (adj.). – Provincial, restricted, narrow – minded, petty, biased.

Parson* (n). – A beneficed member of the clergy; a rector or a vicar; INFORMAL – Any member of the clergy, especially a protestant one.

Pasture* (v). – (of animals) Graze, put (animals) to graze in a pasture.

Patchy* (adj.). – Existing or happening in small, isolated areas; not of the same quality throughout.

Paterfamilias* (n). – The male head of a family or household.

Patriarch* (n). – The male head of a family or tribe; any of those biblical figures regarded as fathers of the human race, especially Isaac, Abraham And Jacob – ------.

Patriarchal(adj.). – Relating to or denoting a system of society or government controlled by men; relating to a patriarch.

Patriarchal*.(n). – Fatherly, kind, a form of social organization in which the father is the supreme authority in the family, clan or tribe.

Patriarchy (n). – A social system that gives power and control to men rather than women.

Peacenik (n). – Informal. Often Derogatory – a member of a pacifist movement, an opponent of war specifically.

Peccadillo (n). – A relatively minor fault or sin.

peckled* (adj.). – Covered or marked with a large number of small spots or patches of color

Pedant (n). – A person who is excessively concerned with minor details and rules or with displaying academic learning.

pedestal* (n). – The base or support on which a statue, obelisk, or column is mounted, used in reference to a situation in which someone is greatly or uncritically admired, idealized, exalted, lionized; (v). – Set or support on a pedestal.

Pedigree (n). – The record of descent of an animal, showing it to be pure – bred; the recorded ancestry or lineage of a person or family; (adj.) – BRITISH (of an animal) Pure – bred.

Peering* (n). – The exchange of data directly between internet service providers, rather than via the internet

Pelf (n). – Fame/money or riches, especially when gained in a dishonest way.

Penchant (n). – A strong or habitual liking for something or tendency to do something.

Penury* (n). – The state of being extremely poor.

Perambulator (n). – DATED. BRITISH – a pram; FORMAL – HUMOROUS – a person who walks, especially for pleasure and in a leisurely way.

Perch* (n). – A branch (or a bar in a cage) where a bird sits; (v). – To sit or be put on the edge of something; (used about a bird) to sit on a branch etc.

Percussion (n). – Drums and other instruments that you play by hitting them.

Perennial* (adj.). – (of a plant) living for several years; lasting or existing for a long or apparently infinite time; enduring or continually recurring.

Perfunctory(adj.). – (of an action) Carried out without real interest, feeling or effort.

Perilous* (adj.). – Exposed to imminent risk of disaster or ruin.

Perilously (adverb). – In a way that is full of danger or risk.

Permeate* (v). – FORMAL – (of a liquid or gas) Pass through a porous material; (of a smell or gas) to spread through a room or fill every part of something.

Perpetrate (v). – Carry out or commit (a harmful, illegal or immoral action).

Perpetrator*(n). – A person who carries out a harmful, illegal or immoral act.

Perpetuate*(v). – Make something continue indefinitely

Persecutor* (n). – A person who persecutes someone, for their ethnicity, religion or sexual orientation or political beliefs.

Persepolis (n). – The city of Persians.

Pervasive (adj.). – That is present in all parts of something, potent, prevalent.

Pervenue. (n). – A person of humble origin, who has gained wealth, influence or celebrity.

Perverse* (adj.). – Corrupt, improper, incorrect, obstinate in opposing what is right; wrongheaded.

Pest* (n). – An insect or animal that destroys plants, insects, food etc., INFORMAL – a person or thing that annoys you.

Pester (v). – Annoy somebody, for example by asking him/her something many times.

Pestilence (n). – Any fatal disease that spreads quickly and kills a large number of people, endemic, infection, outbreak.

Peter out into welter* (v). – Jumble, tangle, clutter, mess, hotchpotch, flurry, rush, to confuse.

Petite (adj.). – Attractively small and dainty (used by a woman).

Petrify* (v). – Change (organic matter) into a stony substance by encrusting or replacing it with a calcareous, siliceous or other mineral deposit; make (someone) so frightened that they are unable to move, horrify,

Phalanx (n). – A body of troops or police officers standing or moving in close formation; ANATOMY – A bone of the finger or toe.

Phallocrat (n). – A male who assumes authority over females due to his maleness.

Phantasm (n). – All illusion, apparition, or ghost; ARCHAIC – An illusory likeness of something.

Phantom* (n). – The spirit of a dead person that is seen or heard by somebody who is still living; something that you think exists, but that is not real.

Pharisaic (adj.). – Self – righteous or hypothetical, relating to or characteristic of the pharisees.

Pharisees (n). – A self – righteous or hypothetical person.

Philharmonic (adj.). – Devoted to music (chiefly used in the names of orchestras).

Pickwickian (adj.). – (of words) misunderstood or misused, especially to avoid offence; of or like Mr. Pickwick in Dicken's Pickwick papers, especially in being jovial, plump or generous.

Piffle* (n). – Nonsense.

Piggyback* (n). – A ride on someone's back and shoulders; (adj.) – on the back and shoulders of another person.

Pigmy (n). – A member of a race of very small people living in parts of Africa and South East Asia; a very small person or thing or one that is weak in some way.

Pilferer (n). – A person who steals things of little value or in small quantities, especially from the place where they

Pillage (v). – Steal things from a place or people by using force and violence, especially during war.

Pillory (n). – A wooden frame for public punishment having holes in which the head and hands can be locked; a means for exposing one to public scorn or ridicule.

Pillory(v). – Attack or ridicule publicly; put (someone) in pillory.

Pinprick* (n). – A prick caused by a pin, a very small dot or amount.

Pirouette.(n). – Make (something) greater by adding to it.

Pitter – Patter (v). – Move with or make a Pitter – Patter sound; (n). – A sound like that of quick light steps or taps.

Pivot.*(n). – A thing on which something turns; specifically a metal pointed pin or short shaft in machinery, such as the end of the axis

Pixar* (v). – Spanish – to make pictures; an American computer animation studio known for its critically and commercially successful computer animated feature films.

Placate* (v). – Make somebody less angry about something.

Plagiarism* (n). – The act of copying another person's ideas, words or work and pretending they are your own; something copied in this way.

Plank* (n). – A long flat thin piece of wood that is used for building or making things.

Plateau* (n). – A state of little or no change following a period of activity, (v) – reach a state of little or no change after a period of activity.

Plateau* (v). – Reach a state of little or no change after a period of activity or progress.

Platitude* (n). – A remark or statement, especially with a moral content, that has been used too often to be interesting or formal.

Plaudit (n). – An expression of praise or approval; the applause of an audience.

Pleat* (n). – A permanent fold that is sewn or pressed into a piece of cloth, fold.

Plebeian (adj.). – From or connected with ordinary people or people from a low social value; lacking culture or education; coarse.

Plethora* (n). – A large or excess amount of something; an excess of a body fluid, particularly blood.

Plomb (n). – surgery – Any inert material inserted into a body cavity for therapeutic purposes.

Plow* (n). – A large farm tool which is pulled by a tractor or by an animal, (v). – plough.

Ploy* (n). – A cunning plan or action designed to turn a situation to one's own disadvantage; an activity done for amusement.

Plummet* (v). – Fall or drop straight down at high speed.

Plump* (adj.). – Someone or something that is slightly fat but often in a pleasant way.

Pockmark* (v). – Cover or disfigure; (n) – a pitted mark or scar on the skin left by a spot or pustule.

Podcast (n). – A broadcast that is placed on the internet for anyone who wants to listen to it or watch it; a digital video or audio file or recording, usually a part of a themed series, that can be downloaded from a website to a media player or computer.

Pogrom (n). – An organized massacre of a particular ethnic group.

Pomfret* (n). – A deep – bodied fish of open seas, which typically has scales on the dorsal and anal fins.

Pomposity (n). – Self – importance; the quality of showing one's own importance; of being pompous.

Pompous (adj.). – Affectedly grand, solemn, or self – important; ARCHAIC – Characterized by pomp or splendor.

Ponderous (adj.). – Slow and clumsy because of great weight, (especially of speech or writing) dull or laborious.

Ponzi Scheme (n). – A Ponzi scheme is an investment fraud that pays existing investors with funds collected from new investors.

Pooper (n). – A person who refuses to join in the fun of a party.

Popping* (v). – Make a light explosive sound; go somewhere for a short time, often without notice.

Portent (n). – A sign of a future event, especially an unpleasant one.

Portentous (adj.). – Done in an overly solemn manner so as to impress, of or like a portent; of momentous significance.

Portico* (n). – A covered entrance to a building, usually supported by columns.

Posit (v). – Put forward as fact or as a basis for argument, put in position; place.

Potlatch (n) – An opulent commercial feast at which possessions are given away to display wealth.

Pragmatic* (adj.). – Dealing with things sensibly and realistically.

Pragmatism* (n). – Thinking of or dealing with problems in a practical way.

Prance (v). – Move about with quick, high steps, often because you feel proud or pleased with yourself

Prat (n). – DEROGATORY. INFORMAL – An incompetent or stupid person; an idiot; INFORMAL – A person's buttocks.

Prattle (v). – Talk at length in a foolish or inconsequential way.

Precinct. (n). – BRITISH – A special area of shop in a town where cars are not allowed; AMERICAN – a part of a town that has its own police station.

Precocious (adj.). – (used about children) Having developed certain abilities and ways of behaving at a much younger age than usual.

Predilection (n). – Preference or special liking for something; a bias in favor of something.

Premonition (n). – A strong feeling that something is going to happen, especially something unpleasant.

Preordained(adj.). – (of an outcome or action) Decided or determined beforehand; predestined.

preponderance* (n). – The quality or fact of being greater in number, quantity or importance.

Preposterous (adj.). – Silly, ridiculous; not to be taken seriously.

Prequel* (n). – A story or film containing events that precede those of an existing work.

Presage* (v). – Be a sign or warning of (an imminent event, typically an unwelcome one, an omen or portent.

Prescient (adj.). – FORMAL – Knowing or appearing to have knowledge about events before they take place.

Presumptuous* (adj). – Confident that something will happen or somebody will do something without making sure first, in a way that annoys people.

Pretense* (n). – An action that makes people believe something that is not true.

Pretzel (noun). – Crisp biscuit baked in the form of a knot or stick flavored with salt; (v) – twist, bend/contort.

Prickle*.(n). – A small thorn; a short pointed outgrowth on the bark or epidermis of a plant.

Prig*(n). – A self – righteously moralistic person who behaves as if they are superior to others.

Primeval (adj.). – The earliest time in history; (of emotion or behavior) strongly instinctive and unreasoning.

Primogeniture (n). – The state of being the firstborn child, the right of succession belonging to the firstborn child, especially the feudal rule by which the whole real estate of an intestate passed to the eldest son.

Primordial (adj.). – Existing at or since the beginning of time or the world; earliest; (used about a feeling) very basic, fundamental.

Prioritize (v). – Put tasks, problems, etc. in order of importance so that you can deal with the most important first; FORMAL – Treat something as being more important than other things.

Pristine (adj.). – Spotless, clean and fresh as if new; unspoilt, in its original condition.

Probity*(n) – The quality of having strong moral principles; honesty and decency.

Proclivity (n). – A tendency to choose or do something regularly; an inclination or predisposition towards a particular thing.

Proclivity (n). – A tendency to choose or do something regularly; an inclination or predisposition towards a particular thing;

Procrastinate (v). – Delay or postpone action; put off doing something, delay.

Procrastination (n). – The act of putting off doing something that you should do till another day or time, because you don't want to do it.

Prod (v). – Poke, push or press something/somebody with your finger or a pointed object.

Prod* (v). – Poke with a finger, foot or pointed object.

Prodigious(adj.). – Remarkably or impressively great in extent, size or degree.

Prodigy* (n). – A child who is unusually good at something.

Profane (v). – Showing lack of respect for sacred or holy things; Technical – Secular; not connected with religion or holy things.

Proffer (v). – Hold out or put forward (something) to someone for acceptance.

Profligate(adj.). – Recklessly extravagant or wasteful in the use of resources.

Profundity* (n). – Great depth or intensity of a state, quality, or emotion; great depth of insight or knowledge.

Profusion* (n). – A very large quantity of something

Progenitor (n). – FORMAL – A person or thing from the past that a person, animal or plant that is now alive is related to.

Progeny (n). – Someone's children; the young or offspring of animals or plants.

Prognosis (n). – An opinion, based on medical experience of the likely development of a disease or an illness. "Most of us take medicines without consulting the doctor. Always good to follow the prognosis of the physician".

Prognosis (n). – The likely course of a medical condition; an opinion based on medical experience, ; a forecast of the likely outcome of a situation.

Prohance (n). – A contrast agent that has magnetic properties. Used in combination with MRI (Magnetic Resonance Imaging to allow blood vessels, organs, and other non – body tissues to be seen more clearly on the MRI.

Proletarian (adj.). Well – balanced, working – class; related to the proletariat; (n). – a member of the proletariat.

Proletariat (n). – The lowest class of people in ancient Rome; (often used with reference to Marxism) working class people especially those who do not own property.

Prolific (adj.). – (of a plant, animal, or person) producing much fruit or foliage or many offspring; present in large numbers or quantities; plentiful.

Prometheus (n). – Greek mythology – "forethought" stands for a God of Fire. Prometheus is best known for defying the gods by stealing fire from them and giving it to humanity in the form of technology, and more generally civilization.

Promiscuity(adj.). – Not restricted to one class, sort or person.

Prop (n). – A stick or other object that you use to support something or to keep something in position; an object that is used in a play, film etc.

Propitiate (v). – Make peace with somebody who is angry by trying to please them.

Propitious (adj.). – Giving or indicating a good chance of success; favorable; ARCHAIC – Favorably disposed towards someone. "Nothing is impossible for a propitious person with positive traits and good managerial skills".

Propitious* (adj.). – Favorable. Likely to produce a successful result.

Proponent*(n). – A person who advocates a theory, proposal or course of action.

Propound* (adj.). – Very great; that you feel very strongly, needing or showing a lot of knowledge or thought.

Prosaic (adj.). – Unromantic, lacking imaginativeness or originality; ordinary.

Proscribe* (v). – Forbid, especially by law, denounce or condemn.

Prosecutrix* (n). – A female prosecutor or plaintiff.

Proselytize (v). – Convert or attempt to convert (someone) from one religion, belief, or opinion to another.

Prosody (n). – The pattern of rhythm and sound used in poetry; the patterns of stress and intonation in a language.

Prostration (n). – The action of lying stretched out on the ground; the state of being extremely weak or subservient, extreme physical weakness or emotional exhaustion.

Protagonist* (n). – FORMAL – (in literature) The main character in a play, film or book.

Protean (adj.). – Tending or able to change frequently or easily; able to do many different things; versatile.

Prototype* (n). – The first model or design of something from which other forms will be developed.

Protracted (adj.). – Lasting for a long time or longer than expected or usual.

Protrude* (v). – Extend beyond or above a surface; (of an animal) cause (a body part) to protrude.

Protuberance (n). – A thing that protrudes from something else.

Provocateur (n). – One who incites another to action.

Prow (n). – The pointed front part of a ship; the bow; the pointed or projecting front part of something such as a car or building.

Prowess (n). – Great skill at doing something.

Prowl (v). – (used about an animal that is hunting or a person who is waiting for a chance to steal something or do something bad) To move around an area quietly so that you are not seen or heard.

Prude* (n). – A person who is easily shocked by matters relating to sex.

Prune* (n). – A plum preserved by drying and having a black, wrinkled appearance.

Pry (v). – Inquire too closely into a person's private affairs.

Psalm* (n). – Song, poem, or prayer that praises God, especially in the Bible.

Psychic (adj.). – (used about a person or his/her mind) Having unusual powers that cannot be explained.

Puddle (n). – A small pool of liquid, especially rainwater on the ground.

Puerile (adj.). – Childishly, silly and immature.

Puffed up (adj.). – Finding it difficult to breathe, for example because you have been running.

Pulpit (n). – A raised enclosed platform in a church or chapel from which the preacher delivers a sermon.

Pulverize* (v). – Reduce to the fine particles; INFORMAL BRITISH – Defeat utterly.

Purge* (v). – Remove people that you do not want from a political party or other organization.

Purging* (n). – Purification or cleansing; the abrupt or violent removal of a group of people from an organization or a place.

Purificatory* (adj.). – Having the effect of purifying or cleaning.

Puritan* (.n). – A person who has high moral standards and who thinks that it is wrong to enjoy yourself.

Puritanical (adj.). – Displaying a censorious moral attitude towards self indulgence, very strict in moral or religious matters.

Purported* (adj.). – Appearing or standing to be true, though not necessarily so; alleged.

Pustule (n). – A small blister or pimple on the skin containing pus.

Putative (adj.). – Generally considered or reputed to be.

Putrefaction* (n). – The process of decay or rotting in a body or other organic matter.

Pygmy* (n). – Something that is very small; (adj.). – used in names of animals and plants that are much smaller than more typical kinds.

Quack doctor* (n). – Who used to sell bogus or out of date medicines, an unqualified person

Quack* (n). – The characteristic harsh sound made by a duck.

Quadcopter* (n). – An unmanned helicopter having four rotors.

Quagmire (n). – A soft wet area of land that has a lot of mud; a difficult, complicated or dangerous situation.

Quail(n). – A small or medium – sized new world game bird, the male of which has distinctive facial markings.

Quaint (n). – Informal – Finance – Short for quantitative analyst

Quaintet (n) – A group of five people who sing or play music together; a piece of music for five people to sing or play together.

Quake* (v). – (used about a person) To shake

Qualia (n). – The perceived sensation of a headache; the taste of wine, as well as the redness of the evening sky.

Qualm (n). – An uneasy feeling of doubt, worry or fear especially about one's own conduct, misgiving.

Queer (adj.). – old fashioned, strange or unusual, mentally unbalanced or deranged.

Quell (v). – Subdue or silence (someone); suppress (a feeling); put an end to (a rebellion or other disorder).

Quench* (v). – Extinguish (a fire).; (satisfy one's thirst) by drinking

Quibble (n). – A slight objection or criticism about a trivial matter; ARCHAIC – a play on words; a pun; (v). – Argue or raise objections

Quiescent* (adj.). – Inactive, inert, latent, in a state or period of inactivity or dormancy.

Quirky* (adj.). – Having or characterized by peculiar or unexpected traits or aspects.

Quisling (n). – A traitor who collaborates with an enemy force occupying their country.

Quiver (v). – Shake slightly, tremble, pulsate, shiver, shudder, agitate.

Quixotic (adj.). – Extremely idealistic; unrealistic and impartial.

Rabid canine (adj.) – A rabid dog or other animal having the disease rabies.

Raccoon (n). – A grayish – brown American mammal that has a fox-like face with a black mask and a ringed tail.

Raiment (n). – ARCHAIC – LITERARY – clothing, attire, garments, apparel, duds, habiliments.

Ram*(v). – To crash into something or push something with great force.

Ramification* (n). – A complex or unwelcome consequence of an action or event; a subdivision of a complex structure or process; Formal – the action of ramifying or the state of being ramified.

Ramp up (phrasal verb of ramp) – Increase the amount of something sharply.

Rampart* (n). – A thick high wall made of stone or earth, usually with a path on top, that has been built around a castle, town etc. in order to protect it.

Ramrod (v). – Force a proposed measure to be accepted or completed quickly; a rod for ramming down the charge of a muzzle – loading firearms.

Ramshackle(adj.). – (especially of a house or vehicle) In a state of severe disrepair.

Rancor (n). – Bitterness or resentfulness, especially when long standing.

Rankle*(v). – (of a comment or fact) Cause continuing annoyance or resentment; (of a wound or sore) continue to be painful; fester.

Ransomware (n). – A type of malicious software designed to block access to a computer system until a sum of money is paid.

Rant* (v). – Speak or shout at length in an angry, impassioned way; (n). – A spell of ranting; a tirade.

Rap* (n). – A quick, sharp hit or knock on a door, window etc.; a style or a piece of music with a fast strong rhythm, in which the words are spoken fast, not sung.

Rapacity (n). – Aggressive greed, avarice.

Rapt attention (adj.). – Showing complete delight or interest; captivated, absorbed, charmed, hypnotized, fascinated, spellbound.

Rapture*. (n) – A feeling of extreme happiness.

Rapturous (adj.). – Characterized by, feeling, or expressing great pleasure or enthusiasm.

Rarefield (adj.). – (used about air at high altitude) Containing less oxygen than usual.

Rattle* (v). – Make a noise like hard things hitting each other.

Raucous* (adj. – (used about people's voices) Loud and unpleasant.

Raunchy (adj.). – Energetically earthy and sexually explicit, shabby or grubby.

Rave (v). – Say very good things about somebody/ something; speak angrily or wildly.

Raven (n). – A large heavenly crow with mainly black plumage, feeding chiefly on carrion; (adj.). – (especially of hair) Of a glossy black color.

Ravenous (adj.). – Very hungry.

Ravisher (n). – A dissolute person; usually a man who is morally unrestrained; someone who assaults others sexually.

Rcklessness*(n). – Lack of regard for the dangers or consequences of one's actions; rashness.

Realignment (n). – The action of changing or restoring something to a different or former position or state.

Realpolitik (n). – A system of politics or principles based on practical rather than moral or ideological considerations.

Realtor* (n). – A person who acts as an agent for sale and purchase of buildings and land; an estate agent.

Rebuttal* (n). – An instance of rebutting evidence or an accusation.

Recalcitrant (adj.). – Uncooperative, refusing to follow instructions or rules; not easy to control.

Receptacle (n). – A hollow object used to contain something; NORTH AMERICAN – an electrical socket.

Recidivist (n). – A convicted criminal who reoffends, especially repeatedly; (adj.). – Relating to recidivists.

Reckless*(adj.). – Heedless of danger or the consequence of one's actions; rash or impetus.

Reckon* (v). – Establish by calculation; consider or regard in a specific way.

Reclaim* (v). – Retrieve or recover (something previously lost, given or paid); obtain the return of; bring (waste land or land formerly underwater) under cultivation.

Recluse (n). – Withdrawal from society, solitude; a person who lives alone and does not go outside to meet others.

Recompense (v). – Pay someone for work they have done.

Reconnaissance (n). – Military observation of a region to locate an enemy or ascertain certain strategic features; preliminary surveying.

Recrimination (n). – An accusation in response to one from someone.

Rectus (n). – Each of a pair of long flat muscles at the front of the abdomen.

Recuperate* (v). – FORMAL – Get well again after an illness or injury.

Redound* (v). – Contribute greatly to (a person's credit or honor)

Reek (n). – A foul smell; (v). – smell strongly and unpleasantly; stink.

Rege (n). – (plural regek) Myth, tale, saga, legend.

Regimentation* (n). – The act of forcing strict discipline and/or organization on somebody/something.

Regressive (n). – (of a tax) Taking a proportionally greater amount from those on lower income; returning to a former or less developed state; characterized by regression.

Regurgitate (v). – Bring (swallowed food) up again to the mouth; repeat (information) without analyzing or comprehending it.

Reinvigorate* (v). – Give energy or strength.

Rejig (v). – Organize (something) differently; rearrange, re – equip with machinery; refit.

Relent* (v). – Finally agree to something that you had refused; become less determined.

Relentless* (adj.). – Unceasingly intense, harsh or inflexible.

Reminiscent* (adj.) – Tending to remind one of something, suggesting something by resemblance.

Remise (v). – Make a second thrust after the first has failed; (n). A second thrust made after the first has failed.

Remission*(n). – The cancellation of a debt, charge or penalty; a temporary diminution of the severity of disease or pain.

Remnant* (n). – A part or quantity that is left after the greater part has been used, removed or destroyed; (adj.). – remaining.

Rendezvous (n). – A meeting at an agreed time and place; (v). – Meet at an agreed time and place.

Rendition (n). – A performance or interpretation, especially of a dramatic role or piece of music, performance.

Renegade (n). – A person who deserts and betrays an organization, country, or set of principles; (adj.). – having treacherously changed allegiance.

Renege (v). – Go back on a promise, undertaking or contract.

Renounce* (v). – To say formally that you no longer want to have something or to be connected with something.

Renunciation* (n). – The formal rejection of something, typically a belief, claim, or course of action.

Repartee (n). – Conversation or speech characterized by quick, witty comments or replies.

Replenish* (v). – make full or replace what has been used.

Repository (n). – A place where or in which things are or may be stored; a place where something, especially a natural resource, is found in significant quantities.

Repost* (v). – Post (a letter or parcel) for a second or further time; post (a piece of writing, image, or other item of content) online second or further time.

Reprehensible (adj.). – Deserving censure or condemnation.

Reprieve* (v). – Stop or delay the punishment of a prisoner who was going to be punished by death.

Reprise (v). – Repeat (a piece of music or a performance); (n). – A repeated passage in music.

Repudiate* (v). – Say that you refuse to accept or believe something.

Repudiation (n). – Rejection of a proposal or idea; denial of the truth or validity of something.

Repugnance (n). – Intense disgust.

Repugnant (adj.). – Making you feel disgusted.

Rescind (v). – Revoke, cancel, or repeal (a law, order or agreement).

Resilience (n). – Ability to recover from misfortune.

Resplendent (adj.). – Attractive and impressive through being richly colorful or sumptuous.

Restive* (adj.). – (of a person) Unable to remain still, silent, or submissive, especially because of boredom or dissatisfaction; (of a horse) stubbornly standing still or moving backwards or sideways; refusing to advance.

Resurrect* (v). – Restore (a dead person to life), revive or revitalize (something that is inactive, disused or forgotten).

Resurrection* (n). – (in Christian belief) The rising of Christ from the dead or the rising of the dead at the Last Judgment.

Resuscitate* (v). – Revive from unconscious or apparent death.

Resuscitation (n). – The action of Making something active or vigorous again; the action or process of reviving someone from unconsciousness or apparent death.

Reticent* (adj.). – Not revealing one's thoughts or feelings readily.

Retinue.(n). – A group of people who travel with an important person to provide help and support.

Retool* (v). – Equip (a factory) with new or adopted tools.

Retrofit (v). – Provide (something) with a component or accessory not fitted during manufacture.

Retroflex (adj.). – ANATOMY MEDICINE – Turned backwards.

Retrograde*(adj.). – Directed or moving backwards.

Reverberation* (n). – Prolongation of a sound, resonance. "Indian marriages present lot of music, dances, delicious food and orchestra with lot of reverberation"

Revile* (v) – Criticize in an abusive or angrily insulting manner.

Rhetoric* (n). – The art of effective or persuasive speaking, especially the exploitation of figures of speech and other compositional techniques.

Rhetorical (adj.). – Stylistic, pragmatic, concerned with effect or style rather than content or meaning; bombastic.

Ribald* (adj.). – Talking about sex in a rude but humorous way.

Rickety* (adj.). – Of a structure or piece of equipment poorly made and likely to collapse.

Rife*(adj.). – (used especially for bad things) Very common.

Rile (v). – INFORMAL – Make (someone) annoyed or irritated; NORTH AMERICAN – Make (water) turbulent or muddy.

Riotous* (adj.). – Wild and full of fun; wild or violent; lacking in control.

Riposte (v). – Make a quick, clever reply to an insult or criticism; make a quick return thrust in fencing; a quick reply to an insult or criticism.

Ripped* (adj.). – (of clothes or fabric) Badly torn; under the influence of alcohol or illegal drugs.

Ripple* (n). – A small wave or series of waves on the surface of water, especially as caused by a slight breeze or an object dropping into it, a type of ice cream with wavy lines of colored syrup running through it; (v). – (of water) form or flow with a series of small waves on the surface.

Riveting (adj.). – Absorbing, captivating, enchanting, engaging, engrossing, enthralling, inciting, extremely interesting.

Roach (n). – INFORMAL – NORTH AMERICAN – Cockroach; a roll of card or paper that forms the butt of a cannabis cigarette.

Roil (v). – Literary – make turbid or muddy by disturbing the sediment; make (someone) annoyed or irritated.

Rooster* (n). – A male domestic fowl; a cock.

Roughshod (adj.). – (of a horse) Having shoes with nail heads projecting to prevent slipping.

Roulette (v). – Make slit – shaped perforations in (paper) especially sheets of postage stamps.

Rudder* (n). – Rugby – A slang word for rugby, or for one who plays rugby football, or a rugby shirt.

Rudderless (adj.). – Lacking a clear sense of one's aims or principles.

Ruddy* (adj.). – (of a person's face) having a healthy red color; Informal British – used as a euphemism for bloody; (v) – Make ruddy in color.

Rudiment (n). – The first principle of (a subject); BIOLOGY – an underdeveloped or immature part or organ, especially a structure in an embryo or larva which will develop into an organ, limb etc.

Rue (v). – Bitterly regret (something one has done or allowed to happen) and wish it undone.

Ruffle* (v). – Make something untidy or no longer smooth, make someone annoyed or confused.

Rugged (adj.). – (of ground or terrain) having a broken, rocky, and uneven surface; (of clothing, equipment etc.) strongly made and capable of withstanding rough handling.

Rummage ((v). – Search untidily; (n). – An unsystematic and untidy search.

Rut (n). – A long deep track that a wheel males in soft ground.

Ryne (n). – An Anglo – Saxon word still in use for a water course or streamlet which rises high with floods.

Sacerdotal (adj.). – Related to priests or the priesthood; priestly; Theology – relating to or denoting a doctrine which ascribes sacrificial functions and spiritual or supernatural powers to ordained priests.

Sacrament (n). – Celebration, communion, baptism, confession, confirmation; (in the Christian Church) a religious ceremony or ritual regarded as imparting divine grace, such as baptism, penance and the anointing of the sick.

Sacrilege* (n). – Violation or misuse of what is regarded as sacred.

Sacrosanct(adj.). – (especially of a principle, place, or routine) Regarded as two important or valuable to be interfered with.

Salubrious (adj.). – (used about a place) Clean and pleasant to live in.

Salvage* (v) Spanish. – Save, rescue, salve.

Samaritan*. (adj.). – Charitable

Sanguine (adj.). – Optimistic or positive, especially in a bad or difficult situation.

Saratorial (adj.). – FORMAL – Connected with clothes or ways of dressing, particularly men's clothes and the way they are made and worn.

Sarcasm* (n). – Derision; the use of words or expressions to mean the opposite of what they actually say.

Sartorial (adj.). – Connected with clothes or a way of dressing, particularly men's clothes and the way they are made and worn.

Sash* (n). – A long strip or loop of cloth worn over one shoulder or round the waist, especially as part of a uniform or official dress.

Satish* (n). – God of Truth, victorious, Sunrise, Lord of Hundreds.

Satrap* (n). – A provincial governor in the ancient Persian empire.

Savage* (adj.). – (of an animal or force of nature) Fierce, violent, and uncontrolled, (of something bad or negative) very great; severe.

Savior (n). – A person who saves someone or something from danger or difficulty; (in Christianity) God or Jesus Christ as the redeemer of sin and saver of souls.

savor*.(v). – Taste (good food or drink) and enjoy it to the fullest.

Savoury* (adj.). – (used about food) having a taste that is not sweet but salty.

Sawder* (n). – Flattery, compliments

Scabbard (n). – A cover for the blade of a sword or dagger, usually made of leather or metal.

Scalding* (adj.). – Boiling.

Scandalous*(adj.). – Causing general public outrage by a perceived offense against morality or law.

Scattershot (adj.). – Denoting something that is broad but random and haphazard in its range.

Schism. (n). – A split or division between strongly opposed sections or parties, caused by difference of opinion or belief.

Schizophrenia (n). – (general use) – A mentality or approach characterized by inconsistent or contradictory elements.

Sciatica* (n). – Pain affecting the back, hip, and outer side of the leg, caused by compression of a spinal nerve root in the lower back often owing to degeneration of an intervertebral disc.

Scintillating* (adj.). – Sparkling or shining brightly; brilliantly and excitingly clever or skillful.

Scion* (n). – A young shoot or twig of a plant, especially one cut for grafting or rooting; a descendent of a notable family.

Sclerosis (n). – A medical condition in which a part inside one's body becomes hard.

Sclerotic (adj.). – Becoming rigid and unresponsive; losing the ability to adapt; Medicine – of or having sclerosis.

Scoff* (v). – Speak about somebody/something in a way that shows that you think that he/she/it is stupid or ridiculous.

Scoop* (n). – A tool like a spoon used for picking up ice cream, flour, grain, etc.; the amount that one scoop contains.

Scoot (v). – Go or leave somewhere quickly; slide in a sitting position.

Scornful*.(adj.). – Contemptuous.

Scour* (v). – Clean or brighten the surface of something by rubbing it hard.

Scourge*(n). – A person or thing that causes a lot of trouble or suffering.

Scramble* (v) – Climbing quickly up using your hands to help you.

Scrape* (v). – Remove something from a surface by moving a sharp edge across it firmly.

Scribble (v). – Write or draw (something) carelessly or hurriedly; (n). – A piece of writing or a picture produced carelessly or hurriedly.

Scrounge (v). – Get something by asking another person to give it to you instead of making an effort to get it for yourself.

Scruff* (n). – The back of a person's or animal's neck; (v). – grasp (an animal) by the scruff of its neck.

Scruple* (n). – Doubt, suspicion, hesitancy, distrust, apprehension, uncertainty, grain of sand.

scrupulous* (adj.). – Very careful or paying great attention to detail; careful to do what is right or honest.

Scuffle* (n). – A short, not very violent fight. “We should live peacefully in the community, since even a scuffle is enough to finish the old relations”

Sculpt* (v). – Create or represent (something) by carving, casting, or other shaping techniques.

Scurrilous* (adj.). – Humorously insulting, making or spreading scandalous claims about someone with the intention of damazing their reputation.

Scurry (v). – (of a person or small animal) Move hurriedly with short quick steps.

Scuttle (n). – A metal container with a handle, used to fetch and store coal for a domestic fire.

Scuttlebutt(n). – Slang – means rumor or gossip. The term corresponds to the colloquial concept of water cooler in an office setting which at times becomes the focus of congregations and casual discussion.

Seamless* (adj.) – (of a fabric or surface) Smooth and without seams or obvious joints; smooth and continuous, without interruption.

Seance (n). – A meeting at which people try to talk to the spirits of dead people.

Seared (adj.). – (of food) Fried quickly at a high temperature so as to retain its juices in subsequent cooking.

Sedition*(n). – Conduct or speech inciting people to rebel against the authority of the state or monarch.

Seethe* (v). – To be very angry; to be very crowded.

Segue (v). – (in music and film) Move without interruption from one piece of music or scene to another; (n). – uninterrupted transition.

Self – abnegation(n). – The denial or abasement of oneself.

Self-effulgent* (adj). – Latin – outshine, radiates warmth and goodness.

Semblance* (n). – The outward appearance or apparent form of something, especially when the reality is different; ARCHAIC – Similarity.

Seminal (adj.). – Inspirational, (used about an article, book, etc.) original, important, having great influence on future developments. "Youths can improve their vocabulary by reading series of seminal books of leaders of their country"

Sensuously (adverb). – Relating to the senses or sensible objects, having strong sensory appeal

Sentient (adj.). – Having the ability to use your senses and to see and to feel.

Sentinel * (v). – Station a soldier or guard by (a place) to keep watch; (n). – A soldier or guard whose job is to stand and keep watch.

Septuagenarian (n). – A person who is between 70 and 79 years old.

Sequel* (n). – Something that happens after, or is the result of, an earlier event.

Sequin (n). – A small shiny round piece of metal or plastic that is sewn onto clothing as decoration.

Sequitur (n). – The conclusion of an inference.

Serenade* (n). – A piece of music or played in the open air, typically by a man at night under the window of his beloved; (v). – Entertain.

Serendipity (n). – The occurrence and development of events by chance in a happy or beneficial way.

Serfdom (n). – The state of being a serf or feudal laborer, slavery, bondage, captivity.

Servile* (adj.). – Wanting too much to please somebody and so obey them.

Servility* (n). – Submissiveness, abject or cringing, subservience.

Servitor*(n). – ARCHAIC – A person who serves or attends on a social superior; an oxford undergraduate performing menial duties in exchange for assistance from college funds.

Shabby* (adj.). – (used about people) Dressed in an untidy way; wearing clothes that are in bad condition; in bad condition because of having been used or worn too much; goofy, scruffy.

Shackle* (v). – Chain, restrain; limit.

Sham* (n). – A situation, feeling, system, etc. that is not as good or true as it seems to be; a person who pretends to be something that they are not.

Shaman (n). – A person regarded as having access to and influence in, the world of good and evil spirits, especially among some peoples of Northern Asia and North America. Typically Such people enter a trance state during a ritual, and practise divination and healing.

Shambolic* (adj.). – INFORMAL BRITISH – Chaotic, disorganized, or mismanaged.

Shamone. (n). – African – American people giving hope to others who see the dark side and think about negativity.

Shear*(v) – – To cut the wool off a sheep.

Shoddy* (adj.). – Made carelessly or with poor quality materials, dishonest or unfair, pointy.

Shoehorn (n). – A shoe horse or shoe horn is a tool with a short handle that flares into a large spoon-like head meant to be held against the inside back of a slung fitting shoe so that a person can slide the heel easily along its basin to the inner soul.

Shoo* (v). – Make somebody/something go away by saying “shoo” and waving your hands.

Shove* (v). – Push (someone or something) roughly; (n). – A strong push.

Shrek (n). – The name "Shrek Is derived from the German word Schrek, meaning 'fright' or 'terror'.

Shrill* (adj.), – High and unpleasant.

Shrivel (v). – lose momentum, will or desire; cause to feel worthless or insignificant; wrinkle and contract or cause to wrinkle and contract, especially due to;loss of moisture.

Shrug* (v). – Raise one's shoulders slightly and momentarily to express ignorance or indifference.

Shudder* (v). – Suddenly shake hard, especially of an unpleasant feeling or thought.

Sickle* (n). – A short – lived farming tool with a semi circular blade, used for cutting corn, looping or trimming.

Silo (n). – A tall tower or pit on a farm used to store grain; an underground chamber in which a guided missile is kept ready for firing; (v). – isolate one department from one other.

Simian*. (n). – An ape or monkey; (adj.). – Relating to or affecting apes or monkeys.

Simmer* (v). – (of water or food that is being heated) Stay just below boiling point while bubbling gently.

Simulate* (v). – Create certain conditions that exist in real life

Sinecure (n). – A position requiring little or no work but giving the holder status or financial benefit.

Sinew (n). – The source of strength, power, or vigor.

Sinicize (v). – Make Chinese in character or form.

Sinister (adj.). – Giving the impression that something harmful or evil is happening or will happen.

Skeptic* (n). – A person inclined to question or doubt accepted opinions.

Skepticism* (n). – The theory that certain knowledge is impossible; a skeptical attitude; doubt as to the truth of something.

Skew* (adj.). – Neither parallel, nor at right angles to a specified or implied line; askew, crooked.

Skirmish(n). – An episode of irregular or unpremeditated fighting, especially between small or outlying parts of armies or fleets; (v). – engage in a skirmish.

Skulduggery (n). – Underhand, unscrupulous, or dishonest behavior or activities.

Slack (adj.). – Loose, not held tightly in position (of business or trade) characterized by a lack of work or activity, quiet.

Slander* (n). – The action or crime of making a false spoken statement damaging to a person's reputation.

Slay* (v). – kill violently; to murder.

Sleight(n). – The use of dexterity or cunning, especially so as to deceive.

Sleuth (v). – Carry out a careful investigation into a crime or mystery; (n). – A person who investigates crimes; detective.

Slew (n). – A large amount of numbers (past tense of slay).

Slobber (n). – Saliva dripping copiously from the mouth.

Slog (v). – Work hard over a period of time; hit (someone or something) forcefully and typically, especially in boxing or cricket.

Sloth (n). – Reluctance to work or make an effort; laziness; a slow – moving tropical American mammal that hangs upside down from the branches of trees using its long limbs and hooked claws.

Slouch (v). – Sit, stand or walk in a lazy way, with your head and shoulders hanging down.

Sloven* (n). – A person who is habitually untidy or careless.

Slugfest* (n). – A tough and challenging contest, especially in sports such as boxing and basketball.

old fashioned.

Slumber* (v). – Sleep; (n). A sleep.

Sly(adj.). – Having or showing a cunning and deceitful nature.

substance across something .

Smear* (v). – Spread a sticky substance across something/ somebody.

Smitten (adj.). – Suddenly feeling love or affection towards somebody; badly and seriously affected by an illness or feeling.

Smother* (v). – Kill somebody by covering his/her face so that he/she cannot breathe.

Smug (adj.). – Having or showing excessive pride in oneself or one's achievements.

Smugly (adverb). – In a way that shows excessive satisfaction or pride in oneself.

Smugness (n). – Excessive pride in oneself or one's achievements. Snap* (v). – Break suddenly with a sharp noise.

Snare (n). – A device (trap) used to catch birds or small animals.

Snarky (adj.). – Critical or mocking in an indirect or sarcastic way.

Snarl* (v). – (of an animal such as a dog) Make an aggressive growl with bared teeth.

Sneaky* (adj.). – Furtive; sly, cunning; (of a feeling) persistent but reluctantly held.

Snear (n). – A contemptuous or mocking smile, remark or tone; (v). – Smile or speak in a contemptuous or mocking manner.

Snippet* (n). – A small piece or brief extract.

Snoberry (n). – Behavior or attitudes typical of people who think they are better than other people in society.

Snoop (n). – A furtive investigation; (v). – investigate or look around furtively in an attempt to find out something, especially information about someone's private affairs.

Snooping* (v). – Look around a place secretly, in order to discover things or find out information about someone or something. Just Think Over – Can you make a sentence using the word "Snooping"

Snout (n). The projecting nose and mouth of an animal, especially a mammal; a person's nose; a cigarette (Informal British).

Snuff* (v). – Extinguish (a candle or flame); trim the charred wick (from a candle); Informal – Kill or put an end in an abrupt or sudden manner.

Snuggle (v). – Get into a position that makes you feel safe, warm and comfortable, usually next to another person.

Sobriquet (n). – A person's nickname, alias, byname, cognomen, epithet, moniker.

Sociopath (n). – A person with a personality disorder manifesting itself in extreme antisocial attitudes and behavior.

Soiree (n). – An evening party or gathering, typically in a private house, for conversation or music.

Sojourn (n). – A temporary stay, (v). – stay somewhere temporarily.

Soliloquy (n). – An act of speaking one's thoughts aloud when by oneself or regardless of any hearers, especially by a character in a play.

Somber* (adj.). – Dark or dull in color or tone; having or conveying a feeling of deep seriousness and sadness.

Sonnet* (n). – A poem that has 14 lines, each usually containing 10 syllables, and a fixed pattern of rhyme.

Sophomore (n). – a second – year university or high-school student; denoting the second recording, film etc. released or created by a particular musician, group, director etc.

Sorcery (n). – The use of magic; especially black magic.

Soufflé (n). – Any of various light sweet or savory dishes made with beaten egg white; a light, spongy baked dish made typically by adding flavored egg yolks to stiffly beaten egg whites.

Spaniel (n). – A dog of a breed with a long silky coat and drooping ears used as a symbol of devotion or obsequiousness.

Spar* (n). – A thick strong pole such as is used for a mast or yard on a ship.

Sparse* (adj.). – Small in quantity or amount.

Spartacus (n). – A person who watches an activity, especially a sports activity, without taking part.

Spartan* (adj.). – Showing or characterized by austerity or a lack of comfort or luxury.

Spasm (n). – A sudden movement of a muscle that you cannot control.

Spasmodically (adj.). – Happening suddenly for a short period of time and not in a regular way.

Sphinx (n). – An ancient Egyptian stone statue of a creature with a human head and the body of a lion lying down.

Spike* (n). – A sharp increase in the magnitude or concentration of something; a thin pointed piece of metal, wood, or some rigid material.

Splash* (v). – Cause (liquid) to strike or fall on something in irregular drops.

Spondylosis* (n). – A painful condition of the spine resulting from the degeneration of the intervertebral discs.

Spooky* (adj.). – Sinister or ghostly in a way that causes fear and unease.

Sporadic* (adj.). – Not done or happening regularly.

Spruce (v). – Make someone or something smarter or tidier.

Spruced. (n). – to make (someone or something) look cleaner, neater or attractive.

Spur (n). – A thing that promotes or encourages someone; an incentive; a device with a small spike or a spiked wheel that is worn on a rider's heel and used for urging a hoarse forward.

Spurn* (v). – Reject with contempt, (n) – an act of spurning.

Sputter*. (v). – Make a series of soft explosives or spitting sounds; (n). A series of soft explosive or spitting sounds.

Spyware* (n). – A computer software that secretly records which website you visit.

Squabble* (v). – Quarrel noisily over a trivial matter; (n). – A noisy quarrel about something trivial.

Squabbling (v). – Quarrel noisily over a trivial matter.

Squalid (adj.). – Extremely dirty or unpleasant, especially as a result of poverty or neglect; showing or involving a contemptible lack of moral standards.

Squander*(v). – Waste (something, especially money or time) in a reckless and foolish manner.

Squat* (v). – Rest with your legs on your feet, your legs bent and your bottom just above the ground..

Squeamish (adj.). – Easily made to feel sick or disgusted; scrupulous; having fastidious moral views.

Squelch(v). – Make a soft sucking sound such as that made by treading heavily through mud.

Squint* (v). – Look at someone with one or both eyes partly closed in an attempt to see more clearly or as a reaction to strong light.

Squire (n). – A man of high social standing who owns and lives on an estate in a rural area.

Squirm (v). – Move around in your chair because you are nervous, uncomfortable.

Squishy* (adj.) – Soft and moist.

Stag*(v). – Buy (shares in a new issue) and sell them at once for a profit; roughly cut(a garment) , especially a trouser to make it shorter; (n). – A male deer, especially a red deer after its fifth year; a social gathering attended by men only;

Stagger* (v) – Walk unsteadily or move as if about to fall.

Stalk (n). – The main stem of a herbaceous plant; the slender attachment or support of a leaf, flower or fruit.

Stallion (n). – A male horse that has not been castrated, or is a slang for powerful and virile man who has a lot of lovers.

Stand – alone (adj.). – (of computer hardware or software) Able to operate independently of other hardware or software.

Stark* (adj.). – Very empty and without decoration; not attractive.

Statism (n). – A political system in which the state has substantial centralized control over social and economic affairs.

Statist(n). – A political system in which the central government controls social and economic affairs.

Statuesque (n). – Sculptures in English towns described on Bob Speel's website.

Steed* (n). – Archaic – Literary – A horse being ridden or available for riding.

Stellar* (adj.). – Relating to a star or stars; INFORMAL – featuring or having the quality of a star performer or performers.

Stench* (n). – A very unpleasant smell.

Stew* (n). – A dish of meat and vegetables, lamb stew.

Stickler (n). – A person who thinks that a particular quality or type of behavior is very important and expects other people to think and behave in the same way.

Stifle*(v). – Make (someone) unable to breathe properly, suffocate, restrain (a reaction) or stop oneself acting (an emotion).

Stigma* (n). – A mark of disgrace associated with a particular quality, circumstance or person.

Stigmatization (n) – The action of describing or regarding someone or something as worthy of disgrace or great disapproval; the action or process of marking someone with stigma.

Stiletto (n). – A small dagger with a pointed blade; women's shoes with high, narrow and pointed heels, the heel of a stiletto shoe.

Sting* (v). – Make somebody/something feel a sudden, sharp pain; (of an insect, a plant, etc.) to prick the skin of a person or animal with a poisonous sharp pointed part causing sudden pain; (n) . – the pain that you feel; when an animal or insect pushes its sting into you; the sharp pointed part of some insects and animals that is used for pushing into the skin of a person or an animal and putting in poison.

Stint* (v). – Supply a very ungenerous or inadequate amount of (something).; (n). – A person's fixed or allotted period of work; imitation of supply or effort.

Stodgy (adj.). – Dull and uninspired; lacking originality or excitement; food – heavy filling and high in carbohydrate.

Stoically (adj.). – Without showing one's feelings or complaining about pain or hardship.

Stoicism (n). – The endurance of pain or hardship without the display of feeling and without complaint.

Stoke* (v). – Add fuel to a fire, etc.; make people feel something more strongly.

Stomp* (v). – Tread heavily and noisily, typically in order to show anger; (n). INFORMAL – (in jazz or popular music) a tune or song with a fast tempo and a heavy beat.

Stooge* (n). – A subordinate used by another to do unpleasant routine work; a performance whose act involves being the butt of a comedian's joke.

Straddle (v). – (used about a person) Sit or stand with your legs on each side of somebody/something, (used about a building, bridge etc.) to cross or exist on both sides of, a river, a road or an area of land, bestow, bestride.

Strait.(n). – A narrow passage of water connecting two seas or two other large areas of water.

Strap* (n). – A long narrow piece of leather, cloth, plastic, etc. that you use for carrying something or keeping something in position.

Strew* (v). – Scatter or spread (things) untidily over a surface or area.

Strewn* (adj.). – Untidily scattered.

Stride (v). – Walk with long decisive steps in a specified direction; crossing obstacles with one long step.

Strifeful (adj.). – Quarrelsome, contentious, polemic.

String* (v). – Hang up a line of things with a piece of string, etc.

Stringency*(n). – Closeness, strictness.

Stringent*(adj.). – (used about a law, rule etc.) Very strict. "The present time is that of management. Stringent behavior of the boss or anyone doesn't work".

Strum (v). – Play a guitar by moving your hand up and down over the strings.

Strut* (v). – Walk in a proud way.

Stunted (adj.) – Having been prevented from growing or developing properly.

Stuttering (adj.) – Progressing in a hesitant or irregular way.

Stymie* (v). – Prevent or hinder the progress of.

Subaltern (n). – An officer in the British Army below the rank of a captain, , especially a second lieutenant; (adj.). – of lower status.

Subjugate (v). – Defeat somebody/something and make them obey you; to gain control over somebody/something.

Subservience (n). – Willingness to obey others unquestionably.

Subservient* (adj.). – Too ready to obey other people; considered to be less important than others.

Subsidence* (n). – Sinking of the ground because of underground material movement.

Subterfuge (n). – FORMAL – A secret, usually dishonest way of behaving.

Subtle* (adj.) – Making use of clever and indirect methods to achieve something; (especially of a change or distinction) so delicate or precise as to be difficult to analyse or describe.

Succinct (adj.) – (especially of something written or spoken) Briefly and clearly expressed.

Succor (n). – Assistance and support in times of hardship and distress; (v) – give assistance or aid to.

Suckling (n). – An unweaned child or animal. .

Suffuse (v). – Spread warmth, color, light, etc. through and all over somebody and something.

Sundry* (adj.). – Of various kinds; several; (n). – Various items not important enough to be mentioned individually.

Sunken (adj. – Below the water – sunken shop, sunken eyes.

Supercilious (adj.). – Behaving or looking as though one thinks one is superior to others.

Supervene (v). – Occurs as an interruption or change

Supplant (v). – Take the place of somebody/something, especially somebody/something older or less powerful.

Supple (adj.). – That bends or moves easily, not stiff, flexible, graceful, elastic.

Suppliant (n). – A person making a humble or earnest plea to someone in power or authority, (adj.) – making or expressing a plea, especially to someone in power or authority.

Supplicate (v). – To beg, to pray; to make a humble entreaty especially: to pray to God; to ask earnestly and humbly.

Surmise* (v). – FORMAL – guess or suppose that something is true without definitely knowing.

Surmount* (v). – Deal successfully with a problem or difficulty.

Surreal (adj.). – Having the quality of surrealism; bizarre; unreal; unusual.

Surreptitious (adj.). – Kept secret, especially because it would not be approved of; secret.

Surveillance* (n). – Close observation, especially of a suspected spy or criminal.

Suzerain (n). – A sovereign or state having some control over another state that is internally autonomous; a feudal overlord.

Swag* (n). – A curtain or a piece of fabric fastened so as to hang in a dropping curve; money or goods taken by a thief.

Swagger* (v). – Walk in a way that shows that you are too confident or proud.

Swaggy* (adj.). – Fashionable or stylish.

Swamp* (v). – Cover or fill something with water, give somebody so much of something that he/she cannot

Swarovski* (n). – A brand name for a range of precision – cut crystal glass which is made only by its producers in Austria.

Swarthy (adj.). – Having a dark skin color.

Swashbuckling (adj.). – Engaging in daring and romantic adventures with bravado flamboyance; (n). – Daring and romantic adventure.

Swathe (n). – A broad strip or area of something; a row or line of grass, corn, or other crop as it falls or lies when mown or reaped.

Sway* (v). – Swing slowly back and forth or from side to side.

Swerve* (v). – Change direction suddenly.

Swiggy* (n). – Harvesting, and festival of food.

Swindle*(v). – Use deception to deprive (someone) of money or possessions; (n). – a fraudulent scheme or action.

Swoon (n). – Go into swoon; (v) – Lose consciousness; feel very excited, emotional, etc. about somebody that you think is attractive so that you lose consciousness.

Swoop* (v). – Fly down suddenly; (used especially by the police or the army) to visit or capture somebody/something without warning.

Sybaritic. (adj.). – Fond of sensuous luxury or pleasure; self – indulgent.

Sycophant* (n). – A person who praises important or powerful people too much in a way that is not sincere, especially in order to get something from them.

Sycophantic* (adj.). – Behaving or done in an obsequious way in order to gain advantage.

Synchronize* (v). – Cause to occur or operate at the same time or rate; adjust (a clock or watch) to show the same time as another.

Syndrome* (n). – a group or signs of changes in the body that are typical of an illness; a set of opinions or a way of behaving that is typical of a particular type of person, attitude or social problem.

Synergic*(adj.). – Working together.

Synergy (n). – Behavior of a system that cannot be predicted by the behavior of its parts; the combined healthy action.

Taboo* (n). – A social or religious custom prohibiting or restricting particular practice or forbidding association with a particular person, place, or thing; (adj.). – Prohibited or restricted by social custom; (v). – Placed under a taboo.

Taciturn (adj.). FORMAL – Tending not to speak very much, in a way that seems unfriendly.

Tambourine (n). – HISTORICAL – A musical instrument that has a circular frame covered with plastic or skin, with metal discs round the edge, to play it, you hit it or shake it with your hand.

Tangle* (n). – A confused mass, especially of threads, hair, branches, etc. that cannot be easily separated from each other.

Tantalize (v). – Torment or tease (someone) with the sight or promise of something that is unstoppable; excite the senses or desires of someone.

Tantalizing (adj.). – Tempting; making you want something that you cannot have to do; tempting.

Tantamount (adj.). – Having the same effect or value as something, especially something bad.

Tarmac (n). – Material used for surfacing roads or other outdoor areas, consisting of broken stones mixed with tar; (v)-Surface (a road or outdoor area) with tarmac or similar material.

Tarry*(adj.). – Like or covered with tar, waste time, delay.

Tattered.(adj.). – Old and torn; in poor condition.

Tattle (v). – Gossip idly; (n). – Gossip; idle talk.

Tawny* (adj.). – Of a yellowish – brown or orange – brown color.

Teeter*(v). – Move or balance unsteadily; sway back and forth.

Tempest* (n). – A violent storm.

Template (n). – A timber or a plate used to distribute the weight in a wall or under a support.

Tenacity* (n) . – Persistence or disobedience.

Tenements (n). – A large building that is divided into flats, especially in a poor area of a city.

Tenet (n). – One of the principles or beliefs that a theory or larger set of beliefs is based on, principle.

Tenuous* (adj.) – Very weak or uncertain

Tepid* (adj.). – (especially of a liquid) Only slightly warm, lukewarm, showing little enthusiasm.

Terfidy.(n). – The state of being deceitful and untrustworthy Indiscretion (n). – Behavior or speech that displays a lack of good judgment.

Terse* (adj.). – Abrupt; sparing in the use of words.

Tether. (v). – Tie (an animal) with a rope or chain so as to restrict its movement

Thaw (v). – (of ice, snow or another frozen substance such as food) Become liquid or as a result of warming.

Theocratic* (adj.). – Relating to or denoting a system of government in which priests rule in the name of God or a god.

Thrift* (adj.). – Careful management, especially of money; healthy and vigorous growth.

Throbbing* .(adj.). – An indefinitely small quantity; a value approaching zero.

Thwart* (v). – Prevent (someone) from accomplishing something; (n). – a structural crosspiece forming a seat for a rower in a boat.

Timorous(adj.). – Showing or suffering from nervousness or a lack of confidence.

Tinker (v). – Attempt to repair or improve something in a casual way.

Tiptoe (v). – walk quietly and carefully with one's heels raised and weight on the balls of the feet

Tirade (n). – A long angry speech of criticism or accusation.

Tomboy* (n). – A girl who enjoys rough, noisy activities traditionally associated with boys.

Tomboyish (n). – An energetic, sometimes boisterous girl whose behavior and pursuits, especially in games and sports are considered more typical of boys than of girls.

Torment (n). – Great pain and suffering in your mind or body; somebody/something that causes this.

Torpedo* (v). – Attack or sink (a ship) by a torpedo or torpedoes; destroy or ruin (a plan or project).

Torrent (v). – Walk with long steps, often because you feel very confident or determined, (n). – A long step.

Torso*(n). – The main part of the body, not head, arms and legs.

Totter (v). – Stand or move in a way that is not steady, as if you are going to fall, especially because you are drunk, ill or weak.

"After drinking, if one totters while walking, it is not safe to drive".

Toucan (n). – A tropical American bird with bright feathers and a very large beak.

Traction* (n). – The action of pulling something along a surface; the power that is used for doing this; a way of treating a broken bone in the body that involves special equipment to pull the bone gradually back into its correct place.

Trailblazer (n). – A person who is the first to do something, or innovator.

Trailblazing (adj.). – Guide, progressive, pioneering, radical, revolutionary, state – of – the – art.

Trammel (v). – Limit somebody's freedom of movement or action, clog, fatter, hamper, manacle, shackle.

Trample (v). – Tread on and crush.

Trample (v). – Walk on somebody/something; damage or hurt him/her.

trance* (n). – A mental state in which you do not notice what is going around you.

Tranche (n). – A portion of something, especially money, a share of something.

Transatlantic(adj.). – Concerning countries on both sides of the Atlantic.

Transcendental* (adj.). – Extraordinary, superior; beyond normal human experience, knowledge, reason or understanding, especially in a religious or spiritual way.

Traumatic* (adj.). – Prevailing, disturbing, psychologically or emotionally stressful in a way that can lead to serious mental and emotional problems.

Travail (n). – LITERARY – Painful or laborious effort; (v). – Engage in painful or laborious effort.

Travesty*(n). – A false, absurd, or distorted representation of something.

Treacherous*(adj.) – Guilty of or involving betrayal or deception (of ground, water, conditions, etc.; presenting hidden or unpredictable dangers.

Treason* (n). – The criminal act of causing harm to your country, for example by helping its enemies.

Tremble* (v). – Shake/frightened.

Tremulous (adj.). – Shaking or quivering slightly; timid; nervous.

Tremulous (adj.). Shaking slightly because you are nervous; causing you to shake slightly.

Trenchant (adj.). – Archaic Literary – (of a weapon or tool) Having a sharp edge; vigorous or inconclusive in style.

Trepidation(n). – A feeling of fear or anxiety that may happen, especially something unpleasant.

Tress (n). – A long lock of a woman's hair; (v) – Arrange (a person's hair)

Triage (v). – Decide the order of treatment of patients.

Tribulation (n). – Great trouble or suffering, suffering, stitching.

Triceps (n). – ANATOMY – any of several muscles having three points of attachment at one end.

Trickster (n). – A person who cheats or deceives people.

Trifle* (n). – A thing of little value or importance; BRITISH – A cold desert of sponge cake and fruit covered with layers of custard, jelly, and cream.

Trilemma (n). – A situation in which a difficult choice has to be between three alternatives, especially when these are equally undesirable.

Triumphalism (n). – Excessive exaltation over one's successor achievements.

Triumvirate (n). – A group of three men holding power/ office of triumvir in ancient Rome.

Triune. (adj.). – Consisting of three in one (used especially with reference to the Trinity.

Trudge (v). – Walk slowly and with heavy steps, typically because of exhaustion or harsh conditions; (n). – A difficult or laborious walk.

Truism (n). – A statement that is obviously true and says new or interesting; LOGIC. – A problem that states nothing beyond what is implied by any of its terms.

Truncated*.(adj.). – Shortened in duration or extent; without its top or end section.

Tryst* (v) – Keep a private, romantic rendezvous with a lover; (n). – A private romantic rendezvous between lovers.

Tuft* (n). – A bunch or collection of threads, grass, hair, etc. held or growing together at the base.

Tumult (n). – A state of confusion or disorder; a loud, confused noise, especially caused by a large mass of people.

Tumultuous* (adj.). – Very noisy, because people are excited.

Turbo* (n). – Short of turbocharger – a motor vehicle charged with a turbocharger.

Turf* (n). – Grass and the surface layer of earth held together by its roots.

Turgid (adj.). – (of language or style) Tediously bombastic or pompous; swollen and distended or congested, unrecorded.

Turret (n). – A small tower on the top of a large building; bell tower, campanile, carillon.

Tutelage (n). – Protection of or authority over someone or something; guardianship.

Tutelary (adj.). – Serving as a protector, guardian, or patron; relating to protection or a guardian;

Tweak (v). – Twist or pull (something) sharply; improve (a mechanism or system) by making fine adjustments to it.

Twig (n). – A small thin branch on a tree or bush.

Twilight (n). – A period or state of obscurity, ambiguity, or gradual decline; the soft glowing light from the sky when the sun is below the horizon caused by the reflection of the sun's rays from the atmosphere.

Twirl (v). – Run around and around quickly; make somebody/ something do this.

Twitch (v). – Give or cause to give a short, sudden jerking or convulsive movement; (n). – A short, sudden jerking or convulsive movement. "The puppy twitches and then lay still on the grassy lawn"

Tyler (n). – Doorkeeper in an inn or owner of a tavern; maker or layers of tiles.

Tyrannical (adj.). – Exercising power in a cruel or arbitrary way, characteristic of tyranny; oppressive and controlling.

Tyranny* (n). – The cruel and unfair use of power by a person or small group to control a country or state.

Tyrant* (n). – A cruel ruler who has complete power over the people in his/her country.

Ubiquitous (adj.). – Present, appearing, or found everywhere.

Uconscionable (adj.). – Not right or reasonable.

Ugnacious (adj.). – Eager or quick to argue, quarrel or fight.

Umbilical (adj.). – Relating to or affecting the navel cord.

Umbling (n). – A continuous, deep, resonant sound; (adj.). – making or constituting a deep resonant sound.

Umbrage (n). – A sense of slight injury or offense, often without reason.

Umpteenth (adj.). – Many times, indefinite number.

Unblemished* (adj.). – Free from unwanted marks or spots like unblemished apples, or unblemished steel.

Unbridled* (adj.). – Not controlled and therefore extreme.

Uncanny* (adj.). – Strange or mysterious, especially in an unsettling way.

Unchaste* (adj.). – Relating to or engaging in sexual activity, especially of an illicit or extramarital nature.

Unconscionable (adj.). – Not right or reasonable; unreasonably excessive.

Uncouth (adj.). – (used about a person or his/her behavior) rude or socially unacceptable.

Underling* (n). – A person lower in rank or status.

Unditry (n). – The expression of expertise in a particular subject or a field.

Unedifying* (adj.). – (Especially of an event taking place in public) Distasteful; unpleasant.

Unicorn (n). – An animal that only exists in stories, that looks like white horse with one horn growing out of its forehead; new metaphorical meaning – it's a start up valued at a minimum of one billion dollars.

Unleash (v). – Cause (a strong or violent force) to be released, release a dog from a leash, relocate.

Unobtrusive (adj.). – Not conspicuous or attracting attention.

Unobtrusively (adverb). – Not blatant, aggressive, or arresting, inconspicuous.

Unpalatable.(adj.). – Not pleasant to taste; difficult to put up with or accept. "One is expected to behave decently at social functions rather than becoming unpalatable".

Unravel (v). – Undo (twisted<knitted, or woven threads; investigate and solve or explain (something complicated or puzzling).

Unrequited (adj.) Formal – (used about love or other strong feelings) returned in the same way by the person you have feelings for.

Unsullied (adj.). – Not spoiled or made impure, not tarnished

Unswerving (adj.) – Not changing or becoming weaker, steady or constant.

Untrammelled (adj.). – Not deprived of freedom of action or expression; not restricted or hampered.

Upend* (v). – Set or turn (something) on its end or upside down.

Upholster* .(v). – Provide (furniture) with a soft, padded covering; cover the walls or furniture in (a room) with textiles.

Upping* (v). – Increasing (a level or amount).

Uptick (n). – A small increase or upwards trends.

Usurp (v). – Seize or hold office, place or function, powers etc. in possession by force.

Utilitarian* (n). – The belief that the right course of action is the one that will give happiness to the greatest number of people.

Vacillate (n). – Waver between different opinions or actions.

Vagabond. (n). – A person without a home or a job who keeps traveling from one place to another.

Vagrant* (n). – A person without a settled home or regular work who wanders from place to place and lives by begging.

valedictorian* (n). – The student usually having the highest rank in a graduating class who delivers the valedictory address at the commencement exercises.

Valiant* (adj.). – Brave, evasive, possessing or showing courage or determination.

Vanguard (n). – The foremost part of an advancing army or a naval force; a group of people leading the way in new developments.

Vapidity (n). – Quality of being boring, boredom, aridity, flatness, dullness, insipidity; the state of being vapid.

Variegated (adj.). – BIOLOGY – Having spots or marks of a different color, FORMAL – Consisting of a lot of different kinds of things or people.

Vassal (n). – A person or a country in a subordinate position to another; a holder of land by feudal tenure on conditions of homage and allegiance, dependent, beneficiary, servant, peasant, slave.

Vassalage* (n). – A position of subordination or submission.

Vaunted (adj.). – Praised or boasted about, especially in an excessive way.

Veep* (n). – A vice president.

Veer (v). – (used about vehicles) To change direction suddenly.

Vehemence (n). – The fact of showing very strong feelings, especially anger.

Vehemence* (n). – Great forcefulness or intensity of feeling or expression; active, energetic, dynamic, vigorous, arduous etc.

Venal (adj.). – Showing or motivated by susceptibility to bribe or corruption.

Veneer* (n). – A thin layer of wood or plastic that is stuck onto the surface of a cheaper material, especially wood to give it a better appearance.

Venison (n). – The meat from a large wild animal.

Vent* (n). – An opening in the wall of a room or machine which allows air to come in, and smoke, steam or smells go out.

Verbalize*(v). – Express (ideas or feelings) in words, especially by speaking out loud; speak, especially at length and with real content.

Verbiage* (n). – Excessively lengthy or technical speech or writing, the way in which something is expressed; wording or diction.

Verbose (adj.). – Using or containing more words than are needed.

Verdant (adj.). – (of countryside) Green with grass or other rich vegetation; of the bright green color of lush grass.

Verily*(adverb). – Archaic – truly; certainly.

Veritable (adj.). – Used for emphasis, often to qualify a metaphor.

Vertigo* (n). – A feeling of dizziness and fear and of losing balance that is caused in some people when they look down from a high place.

Vestige (n). – A trace or remnant of something that is disappearing or no longer exists;

Vestment (n). – ARCHAIC – A garment, especially a ceremonial

Vet*. (v). – Make a careful and critical examination of something; investigate (someone) thoroughly, especially in order to ensure that they are suitable for a job requiring secrecy, loyalty, or trustworthiness.

Vexed (adj.). – Annoyed, frustrated or worried; (of a problem or issue).

Vibe* (n). – A person's emotional state of the atmosphere of a place as communicated to and felt by others; another term for vibraphone; (v). – Transmit or give out (a feeling or atmosphere); enjoy oneself by listening to or dancing to popular music.

Vie(v). – Strive in competition or rivalry with another.

Vied (v). – Contend for superiority or victory (with) or strive in competition (for).

Vigilantism (n). – Law enforcement undertaken without legal authority by a self – appointed group of people.

Vile (adj.). – Extremely unpleasant; morally bad; wicked; of little worth or value.

Vilify* (v). – Say or write unpleasant things about somebody to make other people have an opinion of them.

Virile* (adj.). – (used about a man) Strong and having great sexual energy.

Virulence(n). – The severity or harmfulness of a disease or poison; bitter hostility.

Virulent* (adj.). – Very strong and full of anger; (used about a poison or a disease) very strong.

Viscera* ANATOMY – (n) – The large internal organs in the body, such as the heart, lungs and stomach.

Visceral (n). – FORMAL – caused by strong feelings and not careful thought; ANATOMY – relating to or of the viscera.

Vituperation (n). – Bitter and abusive language.

Vituperative (adj.). – Bitter and abusive.

Vivacious (adj.). – Attractively lively and animated (typically used for a woman).

Votary* (n). – A person, such as a monk or nun, who has made vows of dedication to religious service; a devoted flower, adherent, or advocate of someone or something.

Vouch* (v). – Assert or confirm a result of one's own experience that something is true or accurately described, affirm.

Vulnerable*(adj.). – Exposed to the possibility of being attacked or harmed, either physically or emotionally.

Vying (v). – Competing, contending.

Wade (v). – Walk with effort through water or another liquid or viscous substance.

Waft*(v). – Move or make something move, gently through the air.

Wager (v). – Bet; risk (a sum of money or valued item) against someone else's on the basis of the outcome of an unpredictable event; used to express certainty; (n).

An act of betting a sum of money on the outcome of an unpredictable event.

Wail (v). – Cry or complain in a loud, high voice, especially because you are sad or in pain; (used about things) make a sound like this.

Waltze (v). – To go somewhere in a confident way; to dance waltz.

Wane*(v). – (of a state or feeling) Decrease in vigor or extent; become weaker; (of the moon) have a progressively smaller part of its surface illuminated so that it appears to decrease in size.

Wanton (adj.). – (used about an action) Done in order to hurt somebody or damage something for no good reason.

Warily* (adverb). – Carefully, cautiously.

Warp* (v). – Influence somebody so that he/she starts behaving in an unusual or shocking way; to become bent into the wrong shape, for example as a result of getting hot or wet; to make something become like this; deform, and distort.

Warring (adj.). – (of two or more people or groups) In conflict with each other.

Warthog (n). – An African wild pig with two large outer teeth (tusks) and lumps on its face.

Wary (adj.). – Feeling or showing caution about possible dangers or problems.

Wattle broom.(n). – An Australian shrub or small tree.

Wax and wane* (v). – Increase or decrease in size, number, strength or intensity.

Wearied*(adj.). – Strange or unusual.

Weariness (n). – Tiredness, fatigue, exhaustion.

Welfarism (n). – The principles or policies associated with a welfare state.

Welter (v). – Move in a turbulent fashion; (n). – a large number of items in no order; a confused mass.

Wend (v). – Go in a specified direction, typically slowly or by an indirect route.

Whammy (n) – An event with a powerful and unpleasant effect; a blow, an evil or unlucky influence.

Whataboutery (n). – British – the technique or practice of responding to an accusation or difficult question by making a counter – accusation or raising a different issue.

Wheedle (v). – Use flattery or coaxing in order to persuade someone to do something or give one something.

Wherewithal (n). – The money or other means needed for a particular purpose.

Whet (v). – Excite or stimulate (someone's desire, interest, or appetite); sharpen the blade (of a tool or weapon).

Whiff (n). – A smell, especially one which only lasts for a short time.

Whimper (v). – Cry softly, especially with fear or pain.

Whine (v). – Complain about something in an annoying, crying voice; make a long high unpleasant sound because you are in pain or unhappy.

Whisk (n). – A tool that you use for beating eggs, cream etc.; (v). – Beat or mix eggs, cream etc. very fast using a fork or a whisk, take somebody/something somewhere very quickly.

Whitted (adj.). – Having wit or wits (usually used in combination): quick – witted; slow-witted; dull – witted.

Whiz* (v). – Move quickly through the air with a whistling or buzzing sound; INFORMAL – Urinate; (n). – A whistling or buzzing sound made by something moving fast through the air; INFORMAL – A person who is extremely clever at something.

Whopper* (n). – A large migratory swan with a black and yellow bill and a loud trumpeting call, breeding in northern Eurasia and Greenland.

Whore (n). – Derogatory – a prostitute.

Whorl (n). – A pattern of spirals or concentric circles.

Wield* (v). – Hold and use (a weapon or tool).

Wiggle (v). – Move or cause to move up and down or from side to side with small rapid movements.

Wile (v). – Lure; entice; another way of saying while something away; (n). – Cunning or devious stratagems employed in manipulating or persuading someone to do what one wants.

Wilting (v). – (of a plant, leaf, or flower) Become limp through heat, loss of water, or disease; droop; leave (mown grass or a forage crop) in the open to dry partially before being collected for silage.

Windle* (n). – A measure of corn, wheat, or other commodities equal to approximately three bushels, but varying in different regions.

Wink* (v). – Close and open one eye quickly, typically to indicate something is a joke, or a secret or as a signal of affection.

Wistful (adj.) – showing a feeling of vagueness or regretful longing.

Witchery (n). – The practice of magic, compelling power exercised by beauty, eloquence, or other attractive or fascinating qualities.

Wobble (v). – Move from side to side in a way that is not steady; to make somebody/something do this.

Wolf warrior (adj.). – A diplomacy that describes an aggressive style of diplomacy adopted by Chinese diplomats in the 21st century.

Workaholic* (n. – A person who compulsively works excessively hard and long hours.

Wreak* (n). – The destruction of a ship at sea; a shipwreck; something, especially of a vehicle or building that has been badly damaged or destroyed.

Wrench* (v). – injure part of your body by turning it suddenly, pull or turn somebody/something strongly and suddenly; (n). – A sudden, violent pull or turn.

Wringler (n). – A device such as a mangle weighing water from wet clothes, mops, or other objects.

Writhe (v). – Make twisting, squirming movements of the body.

Writing (adj.). – Turning and rolling your body about.

Wrought (adj.). – (of metals) Beaten out or shaped by hammering, made or fashioned in a specific way.

Wryly. (adverb). – In a way that expresses dry, especially mocking humour.

Wunderkind* (n). – A person who achieves great success when relatively young.

Xenophobia (n). – Dislike of or prejudice against people of other countries; racism; racialism.

Yank* (v). – Pull with a jerk; a sudden hard pull.

Yell* (v). – Shout in a loud, sharp way.

Yonder (adverb). – ARCHAIC . DIALECT – At some distance in the direction indicated; over there; (n). – the far distance.

Zealot* (n). – A person who is fanatical and uncompromising in pursuit of their religious, political, or other ideals; HISTORICAL – A member of an ancient Jewish sect that aimed at a world Jewish theocracy and resisted the Romans until AD 70.

Zealotry (n). – Fanatical and uncompromising pursuit of religions, political or other ideals; fanaticism.

Zombie (n). – A dead body that has been brought to life by magic; a person who seems partly alive, without any feeling or interest in what is happening.

Author's Note

Thanks friends for going through new words and learning a few of them. Keep learning many more words to improve your vocabulary and use them in your day to day conversation with your peers and seniors. Consultation of dictionaries, Google, Wikipedia will be a great help to you.

With Regards and Best Wishes

– Dr. V.P. Gupta

References

1. A. A. Macdonell, H. Oldenberg. F. Max Muller – Translators, The Golden Book of Holy Vedas, Vijay Goel, English – Hindi Publisher, S – 16, Navin Shahdara, Delhi – 110032, India.
2. A. C. Bhaktivedanta Swami prabhupada, Krsna – The Supreme of Godhood by His Divine Grace, The Bhaktivedanta Book Trust, Mumbai, 2019, pp.1 – 796, ISBN 0 – 89213 – 333 – 3.
3. Adam Grant, Think Again: The Power of Knowing What You Don't Know, Viking, Feb 2021, pp. 1 – 320.
4. Google, April 6, 2021 – June, 2023.
5. Jawaharlal Nehru, the Discovery of India, Penguin books, India, 2004, pp 1 – 642.
6. Narendra Modi, Ëxam Warriors", Penguin Random House, India, 2021, pp. 1 – 261.
7. Sagarika Ghose, Indira Gandhi, Juggernaut Publication, June, 2017, pp. 1 – 344.

8. San Francisco Chronicle and SF chronicle,.com, Jan – March, 2022, sections A. B, and C.
9. Times of India, Bhopal Section, April 6, 2021 – May, 2023
10. Vanmali, Inner Traditions, Shiva Stories and Teachings from Shiv Mahapuran, Rochester, Vermont, Toronto, Canada, 2002, pp 1 – 272.
11. Vijay Jhindal, Nitin Agarwal, Pankaj Sharma, 21 Leadership Lessons of Narendra Damodardas Modi, Grapevine India, 2015, pp. 1 – 248.
12. Wikipedia. April 6, 2021 – April 2023.

www.ingramcontent.com/pod-product-compliance
Lightning Source LLC
LaVergne TN
LVHW041159150826
845673LV00001B/215

* 9 7 9 8 8 9 0 6 6 8 7 4 5 *